That Unforgettable Encounter

That Unforgettable Encounter

by
David S. McCarthy

BEACON HILL PRESS OF KANSAS CITY
Kansas City, Missouri

Copyright 1983
By Beacon Hill Press of Kansas City

Printed in the United States of America

ISBN: 0-8341-0834-8

Cover Art: Keith Alexander

Contents

Introduction

While teaching a Sunday School class of young adults, most of whom had attended church activities since childhood, I tried during each session to help students identify with the situation described in the Bible. One Sunday we dealt with an encounter between Jesus and one of His followers. Multiple choice questions were printed on the chalkboard and students were asked to choose one answer to the following statement:

If Jesus met me today He would probably:

a. Chew me out.

b. Give me a swift kick in the pants.

c. Put His arms around me and hug me.

d. Ask if I wanted Him to make me whole.

Result: nearly all the students selected "a" or "b." They felt threatened by an encounter with Jesus and saw the event mostly in negative terms. I wonder if their response isn't typical of many professing Christians?

I'd like adults to think about an encounter with Jesus in fresh, positive terms. Yes, the Lord did speak harshly to individuals and groups during His earthly ministry, but those who received His sharp verbal jabs were cool and detached about spiritual matters. They approached Jesus, not to learn from Him, but to justify their own preconceived notions.

During most of His encounters, Jesus dealt in love with the men and women whose lives He touched. This list included a large number of people whose physical or moral condition made them rejected by society. The message of the gospel is: don't be afraid of an encounter with Jesus. *That*

Unforgettable Encounter is an attempt to show Christians what Jesus did with the people He touched. His encounters reveal important principles that we may apply to ourselves, and in the process we shall find satisfactions that otherwise we might miss. As the believer learns to practice these principles, the daily routine becomes more rewarding; one's life is gradually shaped into closer harmony with the divine plan.

To make the book useful for Bible study groups or for pastors who may be looking for devotional messages to share—perhaps for prayer meeting night—the Scripture passage on which the devotional is based introduces each chapter in the book. But this is not basically a Bible study book; it is intended to be a spiritual-helps volume, for personal devotional reading.

1

Plucking Strange Fruit from a Sycamore Tree

One of the minor characters in my growing-up years was an aged gentleman named John Soule. With his weathered face and snow-white hair he appeared to be the classic New England grandfather; however, he had never married. His declining years were spent in a world that began and ended in the frame house he shared with his sister. An auto accident had left John paralyzed from the waist down, and it took considerable effort for him to use his left arm. On sunny mornings John's sister wheeled him into the front yard where he dozed within a bubble of memories.

And what memories! It was worth the trip across town to hear about his travels as a young man. He seemed to have visited every corner of the world, places that kids knew only from geography books. I was fascinated by his vivid word pictures about cities on the West Coast that seemed a zillion miles away to a sixth grader.

When a born-again experience drew me into the mainstream of church activities, my visits to John's place became less frequent. Attending prayer meetings and evangelistic services didn't leave much time for socializing with senior citizens, but one day I decided to share my faith with someone who didn't have a personal relationship with the Lord. But who needed my witness?

John Soule's image flashed into my mind, and I made up my mind to stop at his house after school. Perhaps I could persuade him to ask Jesus into his life.

John was dozing in his wheelchair when I arrived. He was overjoyed to awaken to company and launched into a spirited account of his European tour during World War I. For half an hour we marched through the campaigns at Château-Thierry, Belleau Wood, and the Argonne, but at last a hush fell over the old man. Quickly, I seized the occasion to talk about my conversion and asked if he would like to make a similar decision. John hesitated, and I leaned forward to catch his answer.

John spoke quietly, weighing every word. "I used to think about my relationship with God, but in the last few years I've put it out of my mind. I've made a lot of mistakes—taken some wrong turns. I guess my life is bent too far out of shape for even God to make it straight again."

I tried to tell John about the Lord loving everybody and that having a bad record didn't disqualify a person from receiving the gift of salvation; but it was useless. His jaw hardened into the set I'd seen so many times before, and I knew John wouldn't give his life to Christ that day.

I wish I'd known more about the Bible. Had I been familiar with the life of Jesus, I'd have read the Bible passage written especially for men and women who, like John, think their lives are "bent too far out of shape for even God to make straight again."

Little Zacchaeus

The story I have in mind concerns Zacchaeus, the notorious tax collector from Jericho. One day Jesus came

10

through town, and Zacchaeus vowed to see for himself what the Nazarene was saying and doing. Catching a glimpse of Jesus wasn't easy, for Zacchaeus was very short, and the crowds kept pushing him away from the action. Eventually the tax collector quit trying to break through the ranks and put Plan B into effect.

Plan B was a sycamore tree on the edge of town, which Zacchaeus climbed. Now he could take in the whole scene. The Nazarene appeared, jostled by curious onlookers; but when He reached the sycamore tree, Jesus stopped and looked up at the little tax collector. Their eyes met and Jesus said, "'Zacchaeus, be quick and come down; I must come and stay with you today'" (Luke 19:5). Startled, the man in the tree "climbed down as fast as he could and welcomed him gladly" (v. 6).

After that unexpected encounter, life could never be the same for Zacchaeus. He promised to give half his possessions to the poor and to repay four times over anybody he had cheated. The account ends with Jesus summing up the purpose of His mission, "'The Son of Man has come to seek and save what is lost'" (v. 10).

Although Zacchaeus was filled with joy, others in the crowd didn't share his enthusiasm. Tax collectors were blamed for selling out to the hated Romans and were reputed to be traitors to God and man. Zacchaeus' Jewish neighbors would always treat him as an outcast, never to be ranked with decent types. Instead they would mention his name in the same breath with robbers and prostitutes, declaring both his profession and person to be *persona non grata*. Jesus suffered fallout from their eruption of bitterness, and the people muttered, "'He has gone in . . . to be the guest of a sinner'" (v. 7).

It's at this point that the passage needs to clutch our consciousness, for there is a principle here for every age including our own. Jesus is willing to risk alienation from num-

11

bers of people just to bring personal salvation to one unloved individual.

Our wonder will grow even further if we focus on that individual. Zacchaeus comes across as a highly successful businessman. He served as chief tax collector in Jericho, meaning that he employed a small force of revenue agents. Since local merchants carried on profitable balsam trade, receipts would have been significant in the tax office. Zacchaeus was an important person in his profession.

Given these facts, we aren't surprised to read that Zacchaeus was wealthy. Apparently, he had used his position to advantage and had accumulated a vast fortune. This, coupled with his rank, should have given Zacchaeus satisfaction and inner security, but peace doesn't come with either prestige or a healthy bank account. Instead, we see the little tax collector seeking a glimpse of Jesus, trying desperately to hear what the Nazarene has to say. Was it spiritual hunger? a guilty conscience? a desire to be treated like a human being with dignity and worth? Perhaps all three drove Zacchaeus into the hostile crowd that day.

The people would do more than merely block the view of Zacchaeus, a man they hated with every fiber of their being. As he tried to see, they would throw elbows in his face and bump him mercilessly until he was black and blue. That he was willing to expose himself to such ill treatment and still not give up his quest to see Jesus speaks volumes about the state of Zacchaeus' soul. Was he driven by a longing to find something that work and wealth had not given him?

One is reminded of a remark attributed to Charles Dickens during the famous author's visit to Washington, D.C., in the 1840s. Dickens complained about "the spacious avenues that begin in nothing and lead to nowhere." How like Zacchaeus and multitudes since, whose lives lack meaning and purpose. Isn't that what Jesus meant when He used the word "lost"? He intended for us to see that a person who strays from the right path will not reach the desired goal; that what occurs in daily life has a spiritual application in our relationship to God.

Zacchaeus has looked for fulfillment in status and riches, but neither has brought satisfaction. When he sees the reflection of his achievements in the eyes of Jesus, he bows in shame and admits, "I'm lost."

Unselfish Christ

We should also take a close look at Jesus' role in this encounter. His only recorded visit to Jericho occurred en route to Jerusalem just a few days before Palm Sunday. The shadow of the Cross was already falling across His life, and Jesus knew that severe testing lay ahead of Him. Most of us, facing similar trials, would be preoccupied with last-minute preparations for coping, but not Jesus. Instead of dwelling on His own situation, He made a special effort to reach out to one more person, an individual that nobody in town cared about.

The Lord's choice of Zacchaeus is even more striking when weighed against His other options. For example, Jericho was home base for a colony of priests and theologians. Within the week, Jesus would need their support as He went head to head against authorities in Jerusalem. Here was one last chance to sway the opinion makers of Judaism; to win support for His mission from influential figures who could argue His case in high places.

Instead of turning His attention to top-level leaders, it's Zacchaeus, the lowest of the low, who receives Jesus' attention. In calling the tax collector by name, Jesus showed understanding of who he was and what he had been, yet the Lord reaches out just the same. He will extend love and acceptance to a known sinner.

13

Novelist Graham Greene has written about a British police official who becomes entangled in a web of intrigue during an assignment in Africa. There is an adulterous affair and the murder of a trusted assistant that fills the official, Henry Scobie, with guilt and despair. He lurches toward suicide, but first he eases into a church to bare his emotions to God. He has come more to curse his fate than to worship, but suddenly there breaks upon him the awareness of One who will not let him go. Overwhelmed by the unexpected persistence of God, Scobie exclaims, "How desperately God must love."[1]

Those words could have been spoken by Zacchaeus, and by men and women who have since gazed into the sympathetic eyes of Jesus. No one, not even John Soule, is so morally bent out of shape that the Lord will refuse to reach out to that person in love. He reads the emptiness of people who are lost and urges them to tap His fullness by an act of faith.

The story ends, not with Jesus' amazing love, but with the radical reshaping of Zacchaeus' life-style. Listen to the man as he springs to Jesus' side: "'Here and now, sir, I give half my possessions to charity; and if I have cheated anyone, I am ready to repay him four times over'" (Luke 19:8). In promising such generous restitution, Zacchaeus was accepting the penalty prescribed by Jewish law for deliberate theft. What a stunning about-face for one who had lined his pockets with exorbitant fees from his countrymen. Strange fruit from a sycamore tree, but as healthy as any ever yielded by those branches.

Nearly 500 years ago, Michelangelo created his famous sculpture of David. The shepherd lad stands, sling and stone in hand, ready to engage Goliath in combat. Historians point out that this masterpiece was carved from a discarded piece of marble that Michelangelo found half-buried in a churchyard. Donatello, another famous artisan, had already cut into the stone, intending to carve the statue of a great prophet. When flaws appeared in the marble, Donatello cast it aside and refused to continue the project. Michelangelo took the stone, flaws and all, and set out to make his *David.* After three years and four months of patient toil, the finished product was unveiled to the cheers of nobility. What had once been rejected and despised was transformed into a masterpiece in the hands of the artist.

Maybe Uncle Sam is looking for "a few good men," but Jesus Christ is out to sign up all the sinners He can find. When He finds them—whether they're leaning over branches in sycamore trees or existing in split-level houses in suburbia—He offers to forgive their sins, take away all guilt, and fill their emptiness with His presence.

Why reject an opportunity like that?

My Personal Encounter with Jesus

Think of yourself as a reporter covering the passage of Jesus through Jericho. What words would you choose to describe Zacchaeus *before* he met Jesus? What words describe the tax collecter *after* his encounter with Christ? Do you find it easier to identify with Zacchaeus before or after he met Jesus? Have you ever prayed to receive Christ as your Savior and Lord? Would you like to make such a commitment now?

My Prayer

Lord, I'm a sinner and I know it. My life is full of guilt over moral failures and wrongs against other people, but the account of Zacchaeus shows me that I can receive forgiveness. At this moment, I turn from my sins and accept Your sacrifice of Christ on the Cross as my forgiveness. I accept Your leadership for my life. Thank You for receiving me "just as I am," and giving me Your salvation. Amen.

2

A Remarkable Case of Give and Take

Few cities in the United States can boast as rich a heritage as Natchez, Miss. In the days when cotton was king, Natchez was the wealthiest small city in the country. At one time, more than half of our nation's millionaires lived there.

Evidence of the towns' colorful past has been preserved in its incomparable collection of antebellum mansions, which were built and furnished by some of the richest merchants of the Old South. Today, Spring and Fall Pilgrimages attract thousands of visitors to Natchez. They come to walk through lavish mansions with names like Stanton Hall, Longwood, and The Elms, a privilege denied ordinary townspeople when the stately homes were occupied by their original owners.

Simon's Supper

Social customs were different in New Testament times, and the curious didn't have to wait until a well-to-do owner died before viewing the inside of his home. The nonwealthy could attend banquets along with invited guests. When a person of importance was invited to dinner, it was customary to allow common people to enter the banquet room. They sat against the wall, close enough to overhear conversation, and they might even exchange viewpoints with the invited guests.

Let's imagine that we're attending a dinner in honor of Jesus. The setting is the home of a Pharisee named Simon. As we step inside, Simon's servants are completing preparations for the banquet. A low table has been placed in the center of the room, but we notice that chairs are missing. Instead, the table is surrounded by slanting couches where invited guests will recline. They will stretch out, rest on the left elbow, and use the right hand to reach objects on the table.

The host is easily recognized. Expensive robes and jewelry mark Simon's wealthy status, while the set of his jaw shows him to be a man who finishes whatever he starts. For tonight Simon has more on his mind than merely hosting a celebrity. We listen to his conversation with the servants and discover that like his fellow Pharisees, Simon is upset with Jesus for breaking strict Jewish traditions and also for claiming authority to forgive sins. Simon hopes to entice Jesus, to provoke Him into some word or action that could be used against Him later.

As guests arrive, each is greeted with the kiss of peace. Since most roads were little more than dusty paths, and shoes were only soles held in place by thin straps, cool water is poured over a guest's feet to refresh them. A few drops of oil placed on the head completes Simon's ritual of welcome.

Then Jesus, the Guest of honor, enters the banquet hall. We are surprised that He is not greeted by a kiss, nor are His feet bathed by the servants. His head is not anointed with oil. Jesus has been snubbed. Simon has resorted to a classic put-down.

The Woman's Weeping

The meal is just getting under way when a woman rises from the outer ring of visitors and makes her way toward the invited guests. A hush falls over the room, for she is widely known to be a woman of the streets. She goes straight to Jesus, standing quietly at His feet. Suddenly she bursts into tears, dampening His feet with her weeping. Impulsively she drops to her knees and uses her hair as a towel to wipe His feet. Like other Jewish women, she wears a small container of perfume around her neck. The substance was very costly, but it was all she had to offer. Quickly she broke the long neck of the bottle and poured the contents over Jesus' feet.

Jesus quietly accepts her attention, causing a smile to play across Simon's lips. This was the break he had hoped for. If Jesus was really the Messiah, He would know about the woman's sin and would have rebuked her. His acceptance of her affection meant either that Jesus wasn't omniscient or that He lacked perfect holiness. The other Pharisees would welcome this information.

Simon hadn't said a word, but Jesus read his thoughts. The Master turned to His critical host and told this story:

"'Two men were in debt to a moneylender: one owed him five hundred silver pieces, the other fifty. As neither had anything to pay with he let them both off. Now, which will love him most?'" (Luke 7:41-42). Simon answered that he supposed it would be the one who was treated most generously.

"'You are right,' said Jesus. Then turning to the woman, he said to Simon, 'You see this woman? I came to your house: you provided no water for my feet; but this woman has made my feet wet with her tears and wiped them with her hair. You gave me no kiss; but she has been kissing my feet ever since I came in. You did not anoint my head with oil; but she has anointed my feet with myrrh. . . . her great love proves that her many sins have been forgiven'" (vv. 44-47).

Moments later, Jesus extended His blessing to the woman: "'Your faith has saved you; go in peace'" (v. 50). Of all

18

the important people at the table, she alone receives His benediction.

As we reflect on the events inside Simon's banquet hall, we are drawn to the unnamed woman. Her actions show us some of the obligations and privileges that come to one whose sins have been pardoned by the Lord Jesus.

We must keep in mind that the woman had already turned from her wayward life-style when she demonstrated her love to Jesus.

In his commentary on the Gospel of Luke, Leon Morris declares, "It is a fair conjecture that Jesus had turned this woman from her sinful ways and that all this was an expression of her love and gratitude. . . . She may have been among the crowds who listened to his teaching and had been so convicted that her life had been changed."[1]

What kind of response do we look for in the person who has become deeply aware of sin, yet has gone on to trust Christ for pardon and victory? For the woman in this incident the appropriate action was a mixture of giving and taking.

Giving

Her giving included *public acknowledgment* that she was a follower of Jesus. To be identified with Him was threatening, for Jesus had already been verbally attacked by the Pharisees and was being scrutinized by Simon and his friends. Did the woman hesitate, wondering whether she would be misunderstood and ridiculed? She decided to take the risk, no matter what the consequences might be. How could she turn her back on the One who had taken away her load of guilt? The question was settled, and she stepped toward the Guest of honor.

In the free world, being counted as Christ's friend seldom carries any threat of physical punishment. On the contrary, most people we know will applaud us for giving public witness to our faith. Even those who make no religious profession admire men and women who stand for the Lord.

We have heard about the imprisonment, torture, and even the murder of believers behind the Iron Curtain. There are places where open identification with the Lord Jesus places one in jeopardy, but these trouble spots seem to be light-years away from our town.

However, many of us know about a subtle persecution that tempts the Christian to back away from open commitment to Christ. Let's call it peer pressure, that psychological vise that tries to squeeze an individual into narrow bounds set by the group. Peer pressure may sometimes work in a believer's favor, but most of the time we see it as part of Satan's strategy to render one's life ineffective for God.

For example, weekend parties may satisfy a young person's normal desire for popularity, but it may be hard to resist questionable activities that take place at these affairs, such as participating in the drinking, drugs, and sexual practices. But perhaps just showing up at such a party could damage a Christian's credibility for the Lord. On the other hand, friends may use persuasion in various forms to bring conformity. When the pressures grow intense, will a Christian teen let peers know that behavior is dictated by one's personal relationship with Christ?

As we grow older, we learn that peer pressure doesn't disappear at a certain age. Businessmen, housewives, professional people all know the pull of a godless society against their commitment to the Lord. As we fight back, we can be helped by mature Christian friends who can support us by their love and prayers. But eventually we must stand alone and make our own decision about supporting Christ publicly.

At age 41, Ronald Mentus faced such a choice. Hundreds of air traffic controllers on the East Coast voted to stage a "sick out" against the Federal Aviation Administration.

"I couldn't do it," says Ron. "I felt obligated to honor my written agreement with the FAA—that I would not take part in such action against the United States Government."

Ron felt that by following his conscience, he was doing what Christ wanted him to do in those circumstances. He tried to use his decision as a forum for witness, but not many people were listening. Ridicule and criticism focused on Ron, and even today some union leaders refuse to speak to him or acknowledge his presence.

"Philippians 4:13 became my foundation," says Ron. "Faith in Christ as my Savior and prayer for His direction were dominant factors in helping me face ridicule and criticism." He adds, "I'd prefer not to endure an experience like that again. But if I do I know I can lean on the Controller in my life, Jesus Christ."[2]

Whether the opposition is physical or psychological, the Christian may overcome by the help of Christ, who always stands with those who stand for Him.

The woman at the banquet gave Jesus something else—a *costly possession*. She brought an alabaster flask of perfume, a globular container which had no handles and was worn on a chain around the neck. The head of the bottle would be broken to release the liquid inside. By using the contents to anoint Jesus' feet, the woman showed visible evidence of the gratitude she felt for His forgiveness.

Men and women in every age want to give their best to the Lord when they consider how much His forgiveness means to them. Andre Thornton, a professional baseball player, expresses what many Christians feel. He says, "As a Christian athlete, I go out on the field knowing that I'm not playing for the fans or for Andre Thornton. I'm playing to glorify the Lord, and I'm doing it in the best way I possibly can. My best is the least I can give to Him."

Your best may involve the use of material possessions for

Kingdom purposes. Perhaps the Lord wants you to use your home for small-group Bible studies or for low-key evangelistic conversations with neighbors and friends. Your car could be used to transport children or adults to services, or perhaps your hobby needs to be given to Christ as a tool for reaching lost people in a unique ministry.

Your best may involve giving a larger portion of your income to local church and world evangelism projects. Bringing one's bank account to the Lord may be just as significant in the 1980s as the woman's gift of perfume in an earlier day.

Your best may mean a larger investment of time in service to God and other people in need. Your commitment to Christ of minutes and hours makes it possible for Him to reach out in caring love to a world that needs what He offers through His people.

The woman in our story showed gratitude by her giving. She gave herself to stand publicly with Christ when He needed her support, and she gave her costly perfume as evidence that her possessions belonged to Him.

Taking

But the woman also received some magnificent gifts from Jesus. "'Your sins are forgiven,'" He told her (Luke 7:48). Actually she had been pardoned before entering the banquet hall, but Jesus' words accomplished two purposes. First, they were spoken in public as vindication of her stand for Him. She was known in the community as a sinner, now she would be known as a *forgiven* sinner. Second, the words of the Lord gave assurance that what she had experienced was real. She could say to herself in moments of doubt, "He said I was forgiven, and I believe it." This public assurance that her sins were gone and would never be brought against her forever must have cheered the woman's heart.

I counsel men and women who are groping for a sense of the *forgiving grace* of Christ. They have asked the Lord to pardon their sins, but the awareness of forgiveness and peace is missing. Sometimes the best answer is instruction on assurance, showing that faith comes before feeling; that emotion is not an accurate barometer of one's relationship to the Savior.

But there are some people who have no assurance simply because they haven't given what the woman in our story gave. They have backed away from Christ instead of taking a courageous stand with Him. They have grasped certain possessions for their own use and refused to bring these things under the control of the Lord.

Since cleansing comes by accepting Christ and not by doing good works, forgiveness may have actually taken place in the lives of these individuals. What is lacking is inner assurance of this fact. I've found that only as these people break away from peer pressure and selfish inclinations to give themselves and their possessions to the Lord do they hear "Your sins are forgiven" with the inner ear of the spirit. Only then do doubts vanish and the men and women know for certain that they have been born again.

Jesus also said, "Go in peace"; literally, "Go *into* peace." This *peace* means to rest secure in forgiveness, knowing that the past is completely erased from the memory of God. His goodwill flows straight into the Christian's life by the power of the Holy Spirit.

The person who is conscious of the greatness of Christ's forgiveness will engage in acts of giving and taking. The giving will come from a sense of gratitude for all the Lord has done, but the taking will come as a surprise. God provides more than we expect, and His last word to forgiven sinners is "Go into peace."

My Personal Encounter with Jesus

Is the Lord speaking to you about actively identifying yourself as His follower? Do you need to stand for Christ at home? at work? in some other relationship? Prayerfully plan some creative ways to publicly declare your love for Him.

Are you aware of some material possession that could be given to Christ as a token of your love for Him?

My Prayer

Lord Jesus, when I think about how much I have been forgiven, it's easy to identify with the woman at Simon's banquet. Like her, I want the world to know that I belong to You, so help me see obvious ways that I can model this relationship. I also want to give You _____, a precious possession that shows my deep love for You. Amen.

3

When Sitting Is Better than Serving

Every spring I find myself counting down the days until our annual vacation. Not only does the extra time spent with wife and daughter tie our family together, but several weeks away from the church gives me an opportunity to hear outstanding preachers. Half an hour on the receiving end of a sermon can be as instructive as reading five books on the art of preaching.

One lesson, reinforced every summer, is the amazing power of distracting thoughts over a listener who is trying to fix attention on the message. Someone has calculated that the human mind receives 10,000 different ideas daily, and on the Sundays I visit worship services, all 10,000 tramp through my consciousness between the opening prayer and benediction.

I can be following the speaker's train of thought when my mind begins to organize the stack of writing assignments and administrative duties back in my study. I usually snap back to attention, especially if the minister tells an interesting story, but only for a few minutes. Then I'm off to the baseball game I plan to attend next week. In my mind I can smell the hot dogs and popcorn. The crowd roars as the batter blasts a high fastball into the gap to score two runners. At least, knowing that people find it hard to concentrate on a sermon helps me to prepare more carefully when it's my turn.

Unfortunately, distractions aren't limited to Sunday morning at eleven o'clock. Just ask any housewife. Thanks to the inventive genius of Alexander Graham Bell and the frantic pace of modern living, her day is split into more fragments than an atom. Men also know the urge to dash off in six different directions at once. Both men and women feel the anguish when loose ends won't come together in the right places at the right time. The tyranny of the urgent gnaws relentlessly at our daily schedule, and we look for clues as to what's really important.

The Bible shows that this isn't a new headache, a spin-off from space-age technology. Jesus ran into a situation that sounds like a scene in modern suburbia, when He visited the home of friends in the village of Bethany.

Mary and Martha Contrasted

Mary and Martha were sisters. Together with their brother Lazarus, they provided a comfortable retreat for Jesus during occasions when His ministry brought Him near Jerusalem. The Gospels report several times when the Master stayed overnight with these special friends.

One day Jesus arrived before the women had completed their household chores. Mary dropped what she was doing and sat down to learn from the Visitor, but Martha continued to rush here and there, finishing preparations for His comfort. As she worked, Martha grew more and more frustrated. The nerve of her sister, failing to carry her end of the load. And Jesus raised no objection when Mary lingered at His feet instead of returning to her duties. At last Martha's resentments boiled over. She burst into the presence of Jesus and exclaimed, "'Lord, do you not care that my sister has left me to get on with the work by myself? Tell her to come and lend a hand'" (Luke 10:40). Jesus replied, "'Martha, Martha, you are fretting and fussing about so many things; but one thing is necessary. The part that Mary has chosen is best; and it shall not be taken away from her'" (vv. 41-42).

Martha's danger is also ours; that the press of daily routine will become so time-consuming that we'll be distracted from "sitting at the feet of Jesus."

"Sitting at the feet of Jesus" is often cast aside as jargon that Christians use in conversation with each other. Although the phrase may be outdated, the basic concept is timeless. Choose different words if you wish: quiet time, communion with God, devotional exercise—the terminology isn't as important as the idea. The Lord Jesus wants His sons and daughters to consciously enter His presence as they read the Bible and pray. In those special moments the believer expresses love for Him, listens to His instructions, and tries to read the correct order of priorities.

Explain all this to Martha and you'll probably hear her say, "That's a nice thought, Master, but I've been put together differently than Mary. I'm an activist, and it's my nature to stay on the run when I'm not asleep. Why do I need to take time out to sit at Your feet? Isn't my service an adequate substitute for sitting at Your feet?"

No, Martha, sitting at Jesus' feet is for everybody. Why is it so important? My experience suggests three reasons.

First, it's important because of what this communion means to the Lord.

Do you mean that He gets something valuable out of the quality time we spend together?

Absolutely.

Remember how He created Adam and Eve for fellowship with himself, and how He called out, "Where art thou?" when our first parents had sinned and hidden from His presence (Gen. 3:9, KJV)? Remember the reason for the whole scheme of salvation? Wasn't it done so that our lost fellowship might be restored; so that God might once again enjoy conscious communion with mankind? Jesus, talking with the Samaritan woman, declared that the Father was "seeking" those who would worship Him in spirit and in truth (John 4:23-24). Amazingly, the bonds of love between our Father and His children bring joy to His heart. When we sit at the feet of Jesus, either in public worship or private prayer, we somehow bring joy to the heart of God.

A *second* reason why spiritual communion is important is the effect it has on the individual Christian. Let me use several analogies to illustrate what a quiet time with the Lord means to me.

I try to take good care of my car and spend time giving it preventive maintenance. No doubt my efforts keep the repair bills down, but eventually the front end needs alignment. Day by day driving causes problems no matter how carefully a car is handled, so regular appointments at the front end shop are necessary. My life is like my car. I try to follow God's will for my life, yet sooner or later my values and attitudes move out of line with His purposes. A quiet time with the Lord brings the spiritual alignment I need to remain effective in my witness for Him.

Older readers may appreciate a second analogy. My grandmother once owned a nonelectric Victrola, predecessor to the modern stereo. Her record player had a crank on the side, and a person would wind up the machine in order to play the wax discs at 78 rpm. The Victrola would play a couple of numbers without attention, but eventually sound would become distorted, and the needle would halt in the middle of a record. When that happened, there was only one remedy—wind up the record player until the handle wouldn't turn another revolution. That's how the machine was designed to operate. Sometimes I feel like that ancient record player. I'm run down spiritually, and the sounds I make are distorted rather than clear notes of Christ's gospel. The Lord needs to turn the crank in my life, and that can only happen when I consciously enter His presence and renew fellowship with Him.

There's a man who rides around town in an old car with a sign "Everything Sharpened That Needs an Edge." The utensils we use every day become blunted, likewise some of the resolves and qualities that make us useful to the Lord lose their edge. Time spent at the feet of Jesus will restore the cutting ability of our lives.

We need to be aligned spiritually to the will of God; we need to be wound up so that we play heaven's music at the correct speed; we need to have our best qualities sharpened so that our cutting edge is felt by the world. These things happen to us when we spend time in the presence of our Lord.

There is a *third* reason why the quiet time with God is important for Christians; consider what the effects of this encounter accomplish in the lives of others. Isn't it amazing how often the Lord uses one's quiet time to bring to mind the people around us who have special needs? He seems to single out the shut-in who needs a visit or a ministry that needs financial aid. We receive impressions about our role in helping these individuals and groups as we wait before God in prayer.

At other times, the guidance of God and His subsequent help seems even more direct. Dr. L. Nelson Bell spent 25 years in China as a medical missionary. During his years of service, the Nationalists and Communists linked armies to attempt a Soviet-style revolution against the hated warlords of south China. Foreigners were mistreated and several Christians lost their lives as the troops moved north. Missionaries were in special peril.

Meanwhile, back in Waynesboro, Va., Dr. Bell's mother

knew more details of each day's conflict than did her son. Reports sent to the States were much more specific than those carried on radio from Shanghai. Mrs. Bell studied the map to chart troop movements and recognized that most missionaries didn't understand their danger. She correctly determined that only the intervention of a trusted missionary colleague who lived near Shanghai would prompt evacuation from the war zone. With these facts in mind, Mrs. Bell dropped to her knees and prayed that the key Christian worker might somehow send word that would be received by the Bells before it was too late.

There is a 12-hour time difference between Virginia and the village in China where Dr. Bell was working. As Mrs. Bell asked God for a miracle, the Chinese vice-consul in Shanghai was sitting at his desk, trying to decide the best method of moving American missionaries out of the interior. At last he decided to enlist the help of the very worker Mrs. Bell had in mind. The missionary quickly went on the air, urging his fellow workers to evacuate the region according to a particular route. Dr. Bell slipped on the earphones of his radio to hear the noon news and received the urgent message from his friend, while 10,000 miles away his mother touched the throne of God in prayer.

When the events of a lifetime are seen more clearly in the light of eternity, we may be amazed at the impact of our prayers on other people. Sitting at the feet of Jesus has value for them, as well as bringing benefits to our own lives.

How Do We Do It?

It was simple for Mary to sit at Jesus' feet because He was physically present, but how does one assume that position today? What Mary did physically, I may do spiritually when I attend public worship or a study group. When the Word is expounded by someone who loves the Lord and I say to Him,

"Speak, for Your servant is ready to hear and obey," I'm following Mary's beautiful example.

That's easier said than done, especially when you have to feed the family and get some of them dressed and into the car every Sunday morning. Most families find it easier to identify with Martha than with Mary when they finally arrive at church.

I've found it helpful to close my eyes during the prelude or opening hymn. I take a deep breath and visualize myself walking up to the front door of the church, all my distractions and problems packed in a big plastic bag. There's a dumpster right next to the door, and I picture myself heaving the bag of "trash" into the container before I step inside the door. As I walk to my seat, Jesus is standing there waiting to meet me. I smile at Him and say, "Good morning, Lord; what would You like to say to me this morning?" This method works for me; try it.

I've also developed the habit of taking blank file cards and a pen wherever I go. If I'm sitting in a worship service or Bible study, I write brief notes about what the Lord is saying to me about my actions or attitudes. In private devotions I may jot down a Scripture reference that captures my attention. The cards are folded in half and stuffed into my wallet where later on I may meditate on the special message God has given me.

A few minutes at the beginning and end of each day are set apart for prayer and meditation on the Scriptures. At that time I review verses and lessons noted on the cards and ask the Lord for help in making these truths part of my life.

From time to time there are special occasions when I may give extended periods to sitting at the feet of Jesus. A couple of hours spent with a well-written devotional book or listening to taped messages will do for me what sitting at the Master's feet accomplished for Mary.

And don't forget spiritual retreats, away from the pressure of everyday routine. One of our friends tells about a weekend when an adult class met at a Christian camp for an in-depth encounter with the Lord. Just before the campers ate their first meal together, the leader read a devotional passage from one of the Epistles. Then he requested that any conversation around the tables not touch the mundane issues of living but focus instead on the Scripture selection. Later, men and women were able to describe what the verses meant to them.

All of these ideas must be employed in a world where distractions run rampant. The pressures of life are real, and they won't automatically disappear before our resolve to sit at Jesus' feet. There must be continuous discipline, a constant neglect of certain things to permit quietness in His presence.

According to an oriental fable, three horsemen were riding through a desert at night. Suddenly they were confronted by a mysterious stranger who told them that just ahead they would confront a dry riverbed. The riders were to dismount and fill their pockets and saddlebags with stones. At daybreak they were to look at the stones, and they would be both glad and sorry.

The riders soon arrived at the riverbed and took a few minutes to grab several handfuls of stones. Then they resumed their journey. In the first rays of the morning sun the men examined their "stones" and discovered they had picked up diamonds, rubies, and other precious gems. As the stranger said, the men were both glad and sorry—glad they had stopped to obey his instructions, sorry they hadn't taken more of the valuable stones.

When we stand before Christ, will we share the mixed feelings of these travelers? Without question, we shall be glad for all the riches gleaned from God's Word; but when we catch a glimpse of the untapped reserves, we may wish that we had spent more time at the feet of Jesus.

I'm glad the Lord placed this account of Mary in the Word, a reminder that sometimes sitting is better than serving—if the sitting takes place at the feet of Jesus.

My Personal Encounter with Jesus

If you should commit yourself to a daily quiet time, what obstacles would you need to overcome? What might keep you from reaching your goal? Could other Christians help you stay on target? Make plans for "sitting at the feet of Jesus" this month.

My Prayer

Lord Jesus, I find it so easy to confuse busyness with spiritual maturity. Give me the wisdom to plan regular quiet times with You, and the inner discipline to follow through, no matter what temptations allure. Help me to grow in this vital phase of my relationship with You.

4

Do Only Squeaking Wheels
Get the Oil?

Serious talk about the end of the world makes most of us jumpy; however, some people take unusual steps to guarantee their safety.

In the spring of 1975, an unknown number of well-off persons in California despaired so deeply of the future that they paid $12,800 each, in cash, to join a secret encampment. Promoters of the venture will only say that the site covers 700 acres in the rugged Cascades, near Mount Shasta. Stocks of food are stored in a large barn, and the little colony has its own water supply. The only access road could be quickly dynamited, and an arsenal of guns is kept ready to ward off intruders. Despite the hefty initiation fee, plus annual dues of $300, the venture has attracted a surprising number of people who want to postpone their rendezvous with doomsday.

That's one reaction to the hardships of end-time living, but Jesus recommended a different approach. The Master was on His way to the Cross when He drew the disciples aside and talked frankly about "'the days of the Son of Man'" (Luke 17:22ff.). Bible scholars disagree about the specific fulfillment of each detail, but they are in harmony about the prevailing

34

mood of the world just before Christ returns. Grim events will mark the close of the gospel age as satanic forces buffet the elect with confusing teachings and physical suffering.

Christ's Method: Prayer

But Jesus offers His people a strategy for coping with these dangers. In His encounter with the disciples He "spoke to them in a parable to show that they should keep on praying and never lose heart" (Luke 18:1). He actually told two parables to demonstrate the importance of talking with God. That His teaching about prayer should come on the heels of His instruction regarding the last days seems significant. For the Christian who faces tribulation, the answer seems to be earnest prayer.

However, prayer should always be according to knowledge, so Jesus told the two parables in Luke 18:1-14 to clear away several common misconceptions. Prayers that enable the Christian to cope with times of stress must carry the stamp of divine revelation.

In the 1950s, filmmakers developed a process for showing three-dimensional movies. To the naked eye, films shown in 3-D appeared fuzzy—as though the focus of the projector needed adjustment. However, when a patron put on the pair of special glasses given with every ticket purchase, the distortions disappeared. Viewers were finally able to perceive depth and make sense of pictures on the screen.

We may think of Jesus' parables about the unjust judge and about the Pharisee and publican as spiritual bifocals that remove fuzziness from our mental picture of prayer. This divine revelation helps us see clearly God's attitude toward our requests and also shows us the human qualities that He is pleased to bless. As we examine these stories, keep in mind that the telling point in each is made through contrast, not similarity.

35

The Unjust Judge

In the first parable, a widow suffers at the hands of an opponent at law who has taken what little the poor woman has. She takes the case to a judge, but he puts her off, again and again. But the widow knows the value of persistence and follows the judge everywhere. When he steps outside his door in the morning, the judge nearly trips over the widow on his doorstep. She hounds him in the marketplace and disrupts his courtroom activities. When he finally returns home in the evening, the widow blocks his path and pleads once more for an audience.

Finally, the judge gives in. "'True, I care nothing for God or man; but this widow is so great a nuisance that I will see her righted before she wears me out,'" he declares (Luke 18:4-5).

Few readers of the New Testament shed tears for the judge in this story. He showed no sympathy for the widow; in fact, his only interest in the case was getting the persistent woman off his back. On the surface it looks like a classic instance of the squeaking wheel getting the grease it needs.

Does that sound like God?

Remember, the point of the parable rests on *contrast,* not likeness. Jesus was teaching that the selfish judge stood 180 degrees removed from our loving Heavenly Father, who holds the interest of His children close to His heart. The whole earthly ministry of Jesus demonstrated God's care for men and women, boys and girls. He never ignores our requests, never turns His back on our asking.

According to the parable, God will act "speedily" (v. 8, KJV) when His people call upon Him. The construction in the original language makes this term emphatic; God moves in love, dealing with the requests of believers when they are made.

For this reason, the widow in Jesus' story represents a contrast to the attitude shown by Christians. She must badger the judge, pleading again and again before her case is heard, but believers are quite different in their approach to God. Since we are talking with a Father who hears our requests when we call on Him, we need not assail heaven with repetitious prayers.

Of course there will be times when a burden is so heavy that one must make repeated trips to the throne of grace to seek comfort, but this is done with confidence that God is working. Faith recognizes that the Lord is actively moving, even when there is no visible evidence that He has heard.

The Christian accepts the fact that God's time for answering a request may not correspond with our time for asking. Experience shows that delay may bring a greater blessing than the more immediate answer; that there may be a distance between our vantage point and the view where God sits. We may not have yet reached the wisdom to ask for what is best, or perhaps our seeking is based more on selfishness than for the greater glory of God.

Whatever the reason for delay, God's people accept the verdict of Scripture. God does care, and He hears every prayer on its first utterance.

A wife left home for a few days, leaving her husband to care for their little boy. During her absence, the youngster moved into his parents' bedroom, but the change did little to quiet his fear of the dark.

"I'm scared, Daddy," he told his father on their first night together.

The father explained that any fears were groundless. What he said was based on persuasive logic, but the silence told him the boy was unconvinced. At last a voice came from the other side of the room.

"Is your face turned toward me, Daddy?"

When the father replied that his face was in the direction of the boy, that he could see everything in the room that might affect the little fellow's security, the youngster dropped off to sleep.

"Is Your face turned toward me?" That's the question we ask of God. The parable of the unjust judge teaches that our Heavenly Father hears us when we pray, and speedily goes to work on our case.

The Pharisee and the Publican

The second parable begins, "'Two men went up to the temple to pray, one a Pharisee and the other a tax-gatherer'" (v. 9). At first glance, the pair look alike. Both men were in the Temple; both stood before God; both sought His fellowship. But there were also several key differences, and that is what the parable is all about.

The Pharisee was a respected member of the community, a pillar of his religious group. He belonged to an order whose members tried to preserve orthodoxy among the Jews. No matter how others violated God's law, a good Pharisee observed every detail.

Make no mistake, this Pharisee was good. He was able to pray, "'I thank thee, O God, that I am not like the rest of men, greedy, dishonest, adulterous'" (v. 11). In his daily dealings the Pharisee was eminently fair. He could never be accused of sexual misconduct, and his disciplined life included both tithing and fasting. He comes across as an upright individual who rendered strict obedience to the commandments of God.

The second man in the story was a publican, a tax collector. The Roman system called for letting contracts in the areas to be taxed. A sum was agreed upon for each region, and whatever was collected above that amount became the personal property of the collector. Since many publicans were notoriously dishonest and amassed huge fortunes by bilking the poor, they were disliked by the common people. Jesus could not have drawn a greater contrast in life-styles than by placing a scrupulous Pharisee and self-serving publican side by side.

In his prayer, the Pharisee said, "God, I thank thee, that I am not as other men are" (v. 11, KJV). He was trying to win God's praise by living a spotless life. We search in vain for a note of praise for God's goodness, or any evidence of humility for what he owed the Lord. He offered neither confession for himself nor petitions on behalf of others. His prayer simply trumpets the message, "Congratulations, God. You have me for an ally."

Then comes the contrast. The tax collector "would not even raise his eyes to heaven, but beat upon his breast, saying, 'O God, have mercy on me, sinner that I am'" (v. 13). The construction in the original language indicates that the publican thought of himself as the sinner par excellence. He saw the sins of others as being negligible compared to his own transgressions. His whole being ached with realization that he had abused God's law. Seeing that he could not sidestep the Almighty, the publican threw himself on the divine mercy.

What happened to the tax collector? Jesus said, "This man . . . went home acquitted of his sins" (v. 14).

The Pharisee asked nothing, confessed nothing, and received nothing. He was content to applaud his self-righteousness instead of pleading for mercy, and he ended up unforgiven. It is to the humble, broken man, whose web of lies about his goodness has been ripped to pieces, who gains cleansing from God.

William Barclay tells of a journey he made by train from Scotland to London. The train passed many dingy dwellings, but at one point Barclay glanced out the window and saw a magnificent white cottage, radiant in the afternoon sun. By the time Barclay returned to Scotland, snow had fallen and was standing deep beside the tracks. The train again passed the white cottage, but this time the famous Bible scholar saw the structure against a different backdrop. While the cottage had glistened in pristine beauty when compared to nearby apartments, it now looked almost grey in contrast to the blanket of fresh snow.

In our praying, we need to compare ourselves with the "snow," rather than the "surrounding structures." When the perfection of God is our standard, rather than human norms and social mores, we will take the stance of the publican. And God will listen to our prayer, for it will then come from a humble heart.

Sometimes we forget this truth as we pray for loved ones who have strayed from God's highest will. It's easy to assume the stance of a defense attorney, citing the good qualities and positive factors of their lives—items that God should consider before He passes judgment upon them. Better that we should come to the Throne with empty hands, seeking only mercy from the Lord.

But let's not forget to come, especially when dire predictions of the future blare from every newstand, radio, and television set.

One winter morning, a lady in our neighborhood put out pieces of toast for the birds to eat. She reports that moments later she saw a blue jay walking off with a chunk of bread. The sidewalk was slick with ice, causing the bird to slip and slide. He made no progress until, as if remembering that he had wings, he spread them out and flew away, still holding the bread in his beak.

The jay's memory lapse reminded our friend that she sometimes failed to use her "wings of prayer" to climb above her difficulties. She dropped to her knees in the kitchen and spread her wings in earnest conversation with God.

I hope I'll remember that little episode, and with it the principles about prayer that Jesus taught His disciples in Luke 18.

My Personal Encounter with Jesus

Do I feel that God "owes me" something because of my good works on His behalf, or because of a sacrifice made for Him? At what point in my praying do I need to seek mercy rather than justice from the Lord?

Should I take another look at my view of God to see if I'm depending on persistence to win a hearing with Him?

What step should I take to demonstrate my trust in God and His concern for me?

My Prayer

Father, be merciful to me. When measured by Your standards, I am always the sinner and need forgiveness. Deal with me in grace. Remind me that You are a loving Father, not an unjust Judge. Clear my fuzzy thinking about prayer, through Your revelation. In Jesus' name. Amen.

5

The Boy with a Picnic Lunch

"How do you feel when confronted by an overwhelming human need?" That was the question an adult Bible study leader put to members of her group. Most responses were to the point and painfully honest.

"I usually panic," said a young woman.

"I just feel inadequate to cope," replied another person.

Several others admitted that they found it easy to back away from involvement with tough problems.

Finally the leader offered her own thoughts. Instead of trying to communicate with words, she produced a stunning color photograph of the Grand Canyon. The camera had captured breathtaking buttes, cliffs, and hanging terraces, all poised on the brink of an immense cleavage in space. Multi-colored bands of strata tapered away into dark shadows, adding dimensions of depth and distance. The viewer's attention was drawn to a ledge where, barely visible to the naked eye, two hikers had paused to rest. The men looked like helpless aliens from another world, insignificant appendages to their surroundings. A hush fell over the study group.

"That," said the leader, "is how I feel about meeting the tremendous needs I see in people's lives."

How Can We Do the Impossible?

The disciples of Jesus must have felt a similar inadequacy on the day a sprawling mass of humanity gathered on a grassy knoll near the Sea of Galilee. Five thousand men, plus women and children, had streamed out of the towns and fishing villages for a closer look at the Miracle Worker from Nazareth. As Jesus gazed at the massive numbers of people before Him, He inquired of His followers, "'Where are we to buy bread to feed these people?'" (John 6:5).

Philip replied that 20 pounds (a working person's wages for about six months) "'would not buy enough bread for every one of them to have a little'" (v. 6). Nobody faulted Philip's math, for the disciples were gazing on human need they could not expect to ease with their own resources.

Eventually, Andrew appeared with a small boy in tow. The lad was clutching a picnic lunch of five loaves and two fishes, which Jesus requested be given to Him. As soon as the crowd arranged itself in orderly ranks, the Master blessed the meager pieces of food and handed them to the disciples. Moments later, the multitude witnessed a phenomenal happening, for the loaves and fishes seemed to multiply in the hands of the disciples. Each person had enough to eat, and 12 basketfuls of scraps were collected when the meal ended. The boy's single lunch had fed many thousands of people.

What Jesus accomplished with the loaves and fishes illustrates an important Kingdom principle that encourages disciples in every age. By His action, the Lord showed that one's personal resources, no matter how limited they may appear, accomplish far more than the owner dreams possible when those resources are handed over to the control of Jesus.

What is the secret? How does this multiplication of our resources become operational in daily living? According to John's account of the original miracle, three steps are necessary.

First, the Christian must recognize several things. For example, there must be a recognition of *needs* that exist in an individual's world. As Philip and his friends looked around, they became aware that men and women were hungry and needed to eat. To be sure, they had no idea how to solve the problem, but they gave expert analysis of a pressing need.

Do you keep a clear eye and open ear for needs in the world around you? Think about happenings in your family circle and the heartaches you know about in your neighborhood and community. What are some of the concerns that tug on your consciousness as you move through the daily routine?

In a devotional guide, the late Halford Luccock mentions a woman who was described by her friends as "a seismograph." They insisted that "she can record a shock all the way from a boy falling from his bicycle across the street to an earthquake in Japan."[1] If we also recognize the tremors and shocks that disrupt life around us, we are moving in the direction of usefulness to the Lord and other people.

Along with a recognition of need, we need to see the *personal resources* God has given us to meet specific problems. Take a quick inventory of your life. What if your gifts look almost as empty as Mother Hubbard's cupboard—isn't that how the loaves and fishes appeared to the disciples? Take courage from the fact that the boy's lunch turned out to be an important resource for blessing the multitude, and that the Lord treated those scanty provisions as such.

What are your resources for meeting the need you have

just identified? A few dollars not already committed to necessities; a healthy body and sound mind; specialized training; hobbies; a kind and peaceful spirit? All these, plus other gifts the Lord will bring to your attention, can be used by His hands. As soon as you recognize both needs and personal resources, you are ready to move on to step two.

Second, the concerned Christian must be willing to relinquish what is clutched in the hand to the control of Jesus. Sometimes the surrender may be costly, and one may struggle before submitting to the request of the Lord.

Picture the lad in our story when Jesus asked for the loaves and fishes. While the Record doesn't reveal reluctance to share, certain thoughts must have raced through the boy's mind.

Did he say to himself, "It's all I've got. I may go away hungry if I do what He's asking"?

Or, "This lunch is so small, it can't possibly have value to Jesus. What good would it do for me to hand it over to Him?"

Remember, at this stage the little fellow had no idea that the Master would use the meal to perform one of His greatest miracles. All the boy had was the request of Jesus.

Sometimes His requests seem absurd. Jesus could do so much more with another person's "lunch," but the longer we argue, the more obvious it becomes that He wants us to relinquish the resource in *our* hands.

That's how Ruth felt when her pastor preached about the need for home missionaries in urban centers of the United States. At age 64, Ruth was eagerly anticipating retirement from teaching in the small South Carolina town where she had always lived. Then came the pastor's sermon, followed by a stirring within that Ruth recognized as the touch of God.

"Oh, no, Lord, not now!" Ruth whispered, but the stirrings wouldn't go away. The teacher relinquished her plans for retirement to the Lord, then applied to her denomination's home mission board for assignment in a northern city. Now in her early 70s, Ruth regularly works 16-hour days visiting hospitals, nursing homes, and door to door near her church. She is finding that relinquishing her plans to God isn't distasteful in the least. Instead there is great satisfaction as her surrendered gifts make a lasting impact on needy individuals.

If there is something in your life that you need to relinquish to God's control, don't pull back from a close encounter with Him. Hand whatever He is asking over to Him, and see if the results don't parallel Ruth's experience.

Third, once an individual recognizes a need and personal resources, then relinquishes those gifts to the Lord, the final step follows. One must rely upon Him to bless the surrendered resource according to His will.

The Christian's yielded resources will not always bless 5,000 as did the little boy's lunch, for God is sovereign, and the results must be left in His hands. Whatever the numbers, we may be sure that the Lord's multiplication will make the resource far more valuable than if it was kept for personal use alone.

To rely also implies that the Christian let the Lord multiply a yielded resource whenever it pleases Him to do so. I have no ironclad guarantee that what I offer to Him will be used immediately, as in the case of the boy in Jesus' miracle. Instead, weeks may pass with little evidence that God is doing anything with my offering. Some dedicated men and women have died without seeing a trace of fruit from their gifts to Him. But faith declares that time is on God's side. In His own way and in His own time, He will repeat the miracle of the loaves and fishes with what we give to Him.

Meanwhile, there is ample evidence that the Lord continues to do the improbable with what we place at His disposal. Jon Sim serves as a case in point.

Jon is a Korean who came to the United States as a theological student, then left the mainland to take up secular employment in Hawaii. At first Jon was content to work at paying off school debts, but then his salary became an attractive incentive to remain outside Christian work. Besides, what church would hire a Korean with little experience in handling an Anglo congregation? Still Jon sensed that God wanted to use the young man's gifts. After a struggle, Jon relinquished those abilities and spiritual resources to the control of his Master.

Meanwhile, the administrative assistant of a large mission board was trying to help a weary missionary in Pago Pago, American Samoa. At the assistant's request, the missionary had listed 24 specific things that were needed to strengthen evangelistic outreach throughout the islands. Almost as an afterthought, the missionary added a 25th request—a Korean pastor who could work with nearly 3,000 fishermen who work the waters off American Samoa. The vessels stayed at sea for three to six months, then put into Pago Pago for several weeks to take on supplies. The sailors were often lonely and plagued with personal and family troubles, but had no one of their own nationality to provide counseling and spiritual encouragement.

The mission executive felt reasonably sure of providing requests 1 through 24, but a Korean pastor . . . The assistant didn't even know a Korean, let alone one with the necessary training.

Back in the States, the executive attended a dinner at the mission headquarters. She was seated next to a charming gentleman from Hawaii, who coordinated the denomination's programs in that part of the world. During conversation, the Hawaiian said, "I wish you could meet a friend of mine in Hawaii, a young Korean who has offered himself for pastoral ministry."

The assistant nearly dropped her fork, as she thought of the missionary's request for that precise type of leader. Within a few weeks, Jon was on his way to Pago Pago to work with the Korean fishing fleet.

Jon had taken the first two steps toward fulfilling our principle. He had recognized a need and his ability to meet it; he had also relinquished his resources to the Lord's control. Now Jon must take the final step and rely upon God to perform a miracle.

Without question, a miracle of the first order was necessary for Jon to touch his countrymen with the gospel. The usual strategy would be to go on the ships as they came to harbor and to invite sailors to Korean church functions. The young pastor found that success wouldn't come easily, for prior to his arrival, a preacher had visited one of the ships without going through proper channels. The speaker had delivered a lengthy harrangue, then given a highly emotional prayer. The vessel sailed out of Pago Pago into a terrible storm and sank, with all hands lost. After that, no captain would permit a Christian near his ship while it was in port.

Jon prayed regularly for an opening, relying on the Lord to use the personal resources that had been yielded for Kingdom service. Months passed and nothing changed.

One afternoon, Jon offered a ride to a pair of sailors who were hitching their way toward town. The men felt the warmth of their common nationality, and Jon discovered one of his riders was a captain. Before they parted, Jon had an invitation to visit the officer on board his ship.

From that opening, Jon received invitations to other vessels. Counseling opportunities developed, and even the families of shipowners started attending the Korean chapel. Recently, the owners and Korean government shared the cost of a Korean Center next to the church where sailors may enjoy recreation and receive counsel with their problems.

Many of the men have become Christians, and Jon is welcome to walk to the waterfront and board ships to talk with officers and crew. What Jesus did with the loaves and fishes is being repeated in the life of Jon Sim in Samoa.

Similar stories could be told of the Master's dealings with men and women of every race and nationality. As our limited personal resources are recognized and handed over to the Lord, He blesses them. Beneath His touch, they accomplish much more than we dare to dream in the meeting of human needs.

What do you have that Jesus can use in His service today? Is He saying something to you about yielding that gift to His control? About putting it to work on behalf of men and women with hurts and heartaches? Are you willing to take those steps, relying on Him to multiply the benefits as He sees fit?

My Personal Encounter with Jesus

Set aside an hour for reflection and prayer. During this quiet time make a list of your personal qualities, skills, abilities, and spiritual gifts. Make another list of your most prized material possessions. Commit these things to the Lord, asking Him to show you how to use one or more items for Him. Is it difficult to let go of certain things on the lists? You may want to show your list to a close friend who may suggest ways that these items can be used to achieve spiritual goals.

Consult your list each day for a week. What impressions are forming in your mind about the way certain abilities or possessions may be used for the Lord?

My Prayer

Lord, it's exciting to think that my limited resources are actually raw materials You want to use to accomplish Your work in the world. Take my learned skills and natural abilities; take my material possessions and use them as You once employed loaves and fishes to bless needy people and win glory for Your name. Amen.

6

Go for It!

Your favorite college football team has just scored a touchdown, but it's late in the fourth quarter and they still trail, 7-6. On the sidelines, coaches and players huddle over the big decision. Shall they kick the extra point and settle for a tie, or try to run the ball into the end zone for two points and victory?

"Go for it!" chants the crowd.

The fans know that there's more risk involved in a running play or pass, but this dimension adds excitement to the game and makes a win more satisfying.

While the Bible is silent about football, Scripture does relate the exploits of men and women who accepted God's challenge to "go for it." Hebrews 11 names a bevy of Old Testament figures who took great risks to obey the Lord. In the New Testament, individuals like Peter showed similar courage against long odds.

Peter. There was a man who would never punt in "fourth down and a yard to go" situations. Risk marked many of his achievements, including one time when he tried to walk across the water to Jesus. Let's replay Peter's special encounter with Jesus on the Sea of Galilee. As we examine the account in Matthew 14, we'll watch for *four principles* about bold venturing in the will of God.

Difficulties

First, notice how the urge to take a step of faith often rises when a person is engulfed with problems.

A few hours earlier the disciples had served supper to 5,000 men, plus women and children. Then Jesus sent the Twelve to the other side of the Sea of Galilee. They were following their Master's instructions to the letter when angry winds and waves began to pound the small vessel. By the fourth watch of the night (between three and six o'clock in the morning), the bone-weary disciples were straining to keep their craft afloat.

Suddenly, the men noticed a shape moving across the water. Wasn't it enough that they had to deal with the public all day and struggle against the elements most of the night? Now, on top of everything else, they were about to be attacked by a ghost. How bad does life have to get before a person sees some improvement? When seen against these circumstances, Peter's risk-taking faith takes on added splendor. He recognized that the Figure on the water was Jesus, so he shouted above the storm, "'Lord, if it is you, tell me to come to you over the water'" (Matt. 14:28). His urge to "go for it" actually grew stronger because of the difficulty.

History reports the heroics of men and women who, like Peter, found themselves nearly swamped by violent circumstances. World-evangelism agencies have been founded by persons whose dreams were nearly destroyed by financial pressures. Other founders of key ministries wrestled with physical infirmities. Today, names like Hudson Taylor, Cameron Townsend, and Bob Pierce are recognized in many parts of the world, but their early efforts for God met stiff opposition.

Sometimes the risk is associated with death for the cause of Christ. Jim and Marti Hefley document many cases of torture and murder in their book *By Their Blood: Christian Martyrs of the Twentieth Century* (Mott Media). Most of the martyrdoms reported by the Hefleys have a common denominator. Each victim seemed determined to risk everything for Christ, even life itself.

Perhaps we aren't justified in saying that dangerous circumstances *create* bold faith, but they certainly provide the setting for faith to make an impact on the world.

Writing years later, Peter links trials and faith in this way: "Even gold passes through the assayer's fire, and more precious than perishable gold is faith which has stood the test. These trials come so that your faith may prove itself worthy of all praise, glory, and honour when Jesus Christ is revealed" (1 Pet. 1:7).

Instead of complaining when storms interrupt our tranquility, we should rejoice. Difficult times may actually trigger this urge to take a momentous step of faith, resulting in blessing to ourselves and others.

Direction

But let's return to Matthew 14, where a second principle stands out. As soon as Jesus disclosed His identity, Peter asked for permission to walk across the water to Jesus.

"Come," the Lord replied.

Peter risked everything when he climbed overboard, but his faith rested on a word from Jesus. Those who determine to "go for it" need a clear signal that their actions are in line with the will of God.

As a young person in high school, I spent many hours mapping plans for college and a career. After making several false starts, I felt impressed to attend Bible school and enter the ministry, but my grandmother offered sobering counsel.

"Make sure that you get the mind of the Lord on this matter before you finally decide," she warned. A committed Christian, Grammy was eager to see her grandson active in the Lord's work, but she wanted to be sure that my venture was prompted by God rather than a personal whim.

"There will be times of discouragement when you will wonder why you made such a foolish choice," she continued. "That's when you need to know that the decision started with God."

I've learned that Grammy was right. I've also discovered that getting clear signals from God is important at every level of decision-making.

How one finds the will of God on a matter is a subject requiring longer treatment than is possible here. However, I believe that the Lord will disclose His mind to anyone who seeks Him with sincerity and an obedient spirit. Details of that guidance may vary from person to person. Sometimes it comes through Spirit-filled Christian friends or a devotional book. At other times the Lord may use a sermon, or impress a Bible passage on the seeker. All who sincerely want guidance may count on receiving it in some fashion, even though it seldom arrives as a vision or an audible voice from another world.

Are you considering a bold venture for God? Ask yourself, What will I claim from Him if my risk-taking runs into trouble? When I seem to make no headway against the storm, what will I cling to? Your answers may help you to determine whether to "go for it" is God's idea or an ill-fated ego trip.

Danger

I've already hinted at the third principle in our story. When a person steps out on faith, that individual should expect to face danger. Notice that the winds and waves didn't quit their relentless pounding when Peter's foot hit the water.

The fact is, things quickly went from bad to worse for the fisherman. At least he had a few timbers between himself and the sea while he was in the boat, but once over the side he was exposed directly to the elements.

Let the person who decides to venture at God's bidding know in advance that difficulties will likely mount on every hand. Many Christians have not anticipated the problems that will develop and have been untracked from their original goals. You may find yourself numbered among those who have surrendered to the winds and waves unless you fix your gaze on the Lord.

Let's call her Judy. She's a middle-aged homemaker who also works as a secretary in the southwestern United States. Judy has thought of herself as a Christian for many years, but recently she made a deeper commitment to the Lord. Now she's looking for opportunities to share her faith.

One noon, Judy discovered that a girl in her office was having serious problems with her husband. Judy tried to be a sympathetic listener that day, but silently she wondered if she could say anything that would help the situation. Later, at home, Judy felt a strong urge to tell her friend about the plus of a relationship with Christ. Eventually Judy made an appointment with the girl so that she could share her faith.

During the meeting, Judy's hands trembled as she turned the pages of her Bible. Never before had she given her personal testimony or invited another individual to trust Christ. Despite Judy's jitters, the Lord seemed to enter the room and give the conversation a deeper dimension. Before the girls parted, Judy's friend had made a commitment to Christ.

The girl's decision gave Judy a thrill. The Lord also brought healing into the troubled marriage, and plans for divorce seemed to evaporate. Both the girl and her husband began attending church activities. But that's only part of the story.

The new convert leans heavily on Judy for support. When the girl developed a hunger for Bible study, Judy gave up her lunch hour several times a week to explain certain passages and run over the basics of Christian living. In addition, there are usually phone calls for spiritual counseling after Judy gets home at night.

"I'm amazed at the extra work involved in helping a new Christian grow toward maturity," Judy reports. "I thought my biggest risk would be sharing my faith that first night, but now I feel like Peter every time I see my friend. Working with her takes so much time—and all those questions!"

Hopefully, Judy will weather the storm. She knows that Peter started well when he tried to walk to Jesus, but when he became too occupied with circumstances, he began to sink.

So far we've seen that risk taking may become an attractive option for us when we face insurmountable troubles, that the Christian needs to claim a word from the Lord before launching a bold venture, and that once we take a risk we may expect to encounter dangers.

Despair

Finally, we need to consider what happens when the risk-taker succumbs to negative circumstances. "Beginning to sink, he cried, 'Save me, Lord.' Jesus at once reached out and caught hold of him" (Matt. 14:30-31). Jesus seized the sinking man and walked him to the ship. There, the Lord talked to all the disciples about the need for faith in order to be strong.

That story of the rescuing Christ is Peter's testimony, but it's also your story and mine. We need to know that when we take risks, prompted by the Savior, that He remains close at hand to catch us if we grow weak. He picks us up, gently reprimands us, and helps us to walk with Him.

Elisabeth Elliot, a writer whose recounting of personal experiences has helped many readers, recalls her years in Ecuador when she often depended on the services of a guide.

> I usually traveled on foot. And trails often led through streams and rivers which we had to wade, but sometimes there was a log laid high above the water which we had to cross.
>
> I dreaded those logs and was often tempted to take the steep, hard way down to the ravine and up the other side. But the Indians would say, "Just walk across, senorita," and over they would go, confident and light-footed.... On the log I could not keep from looking down at the river below. I knew I would slip. I had never been any good at balancing myself on the tops of walls and things, and the log looked impossible. So my guide would stretch out a hand, and the touch of it was all I needed. I stopped worrying about slipping. I stopped looking down at the river or even at the log and looked at the guide, who held my hand with only the lightest touch.... His being there and his touch were all that I needed.
>
> The analogy breaks down, of course. If our guide is God, He can hold us from any slipping.... But the lesson the Lord taught me was that of trust. ... God's hand reaches toward me. I have only to take it.[1]

In the final analysis, risk always involves trust. For the Christian that trust is focused on Jesus Christ. It is He who gives us the urge to "go for it." It is He who prompts us to step into a dark unknown; and when we become more aware of the dangers, He stands by our side to steady us. He is there to reach out and catch us if we fail to stand against the storm.

"Go for it"—with your eyes fixed on Him.

My Personal Encounter with Jesus

Is there an experience that I've been avoiding because, quite frankly, I'm afraid to take the risk? What makes me feel that the Lord may be prompting me to take that risk and venture out in His strength? What are the "winds and waves" that might swamp me if I take such a step? Suppose I stumble, how will I remember that Christ stands ready to catch me?

My Prayer

Lord, as I think about the risks You might want me to take, I'm timid. I'd rather stay in the relative security and complain about the weather outside, but I'm willing to follow Your prompting and "go for it." Just remind me when I see the dangers that You are close at hand to help me. When I get in over my head, I want to feel Your touch. Amen.

7

Stormy Weather, Steadying Hand

Battling a gale on the North Atlantic gives one proper respect for the awesome forces of nature. Wind-whipped swells may become so gigantic that when a vessel bottoms out in a trough, the wave behind it rises higher than the mast. At times a ship seems no more secure than a reed raft tossed about on a rolling ocean. Veteran sailors insist that nothing saps a person's energy like the relentless slashing of mountainous seas. A man whose fingers ache from grasping the bulwarks for hours may wonder if he will ever see his loved ones again. Even rescue by air sometimes looks impossible.

Foul weather provides preachers and poets with ample illustrations of the unpleasant experiences that come to us all sooner or later. *Storms of life* may be an overworked cliche, but it would be hard to picture adversity with greater accuracy. Hymn writers are especially fond of imagery from the pounding surf. Can we recall the song "Jesus, Savior, pilot me / Over life's tempestuous sea"? Or, "Tho' the angry surges roll / On my tempest-driven soul ... my anchor holds"? Although these lyrics were written many years ago, they express a timeless truth. Life can brew some savage winds and high tides that explode against us with the impact of a level-five hurricane. No one is completely exempt from danger.

Come to think about it, Jesus used the same figure in His parable about the two builders who erected houses on different types of foundation. The storm that followed their construction work showed one man to be wise, the other foolish.

Make no mistake, Jesus knew about storms from first-hand experience. Matthew, Mark, and Luke all tell about the night when the Master and His disciples were beset by a raging tempest on the Sea of Galilee. The day had been filled with emotion-draining activities before Jesus ever set foot in the small vessel. He had healed a demon-possessed man, dealt with opposition from His friends as well as the fury of His foes. In addition, He had probably preached several times. No wonder that as soon as He came on board, Jesus laid His head on the rower's leather seat in the stern and fell asleep.

After dark, a storm roared down the lake, churning the water into unmanageable turbulence. At first the disciples bailed water from the ship and left Jesus alone, then they panicked. We hear the desperation in their tone as they nearly shouted, "Don't You care that we're drowning?"

Jesus stood up, "rebuked the wind, and said to the sea, 'Hush! Be still!' The wind dropped and there was a dead calm" (Mark 4:39). It isn't hard to see *several similarities* between the storm on *Galilee* and the severe testings that rage against the *human spirit.*

Suddenness

We notice that both natural storms and adversity have a tendency to occur suddenly, without warning.

The Sea of Galilee, shaped like a human heart, is one of the most beautiful spots in the Holy Land. It lies nestled among green, enfolding hills, seldom showing its dangerous side. However, the atmosphere is still and heavy, and as colder currents sweep in from the west, they are sucked down in whirlpools of air. Mammoth waves begin to break across the lake, and in a matter of moments the calm sea is transformed into a boiling, raging fury.

Despite sophisticated equipment and the application of modern techniques, scientists are often startled by earthquakes, storms, and volcanic eruptions. When Mount Saint Helens exploded for the fourth time in July, 1980, geologists who were monitoring the situation were stunned. "Yesterday we didn't expect anything like this to happen," said one scientist on the evening of the explosion. "In fact, even today we weren't looking for anything like this."

"Unexpected" is a good word to keep in mind when thinking about natural phenomena. It's also a useful term when we try to cope with the harsh realities of life, for bad news frequently comes without warning. A bulletin on television, the unexpected letter, a jangling telephone at three o'clock in the morning—these signal the arrival of adversity. If only the news came at a better time, if only it approached when we were rested, well fed, able to cope. If only ... But adversity, like storms, usually comes suddenly.

Fears

As a pastor, I've learned that storms in the spiritual realm, like those in nature, produce deep-seated fears. The disciples must have gone through a terrifying time that night on the lake. The roar of powerful breakers, coupled with the sight of waves looming like shadows, would trigger feelings of dread in anyone. In a similar way, bad news strikes terror in the human spirit. At times I've felt like someone was twisting a sharp-edged ball of fear inside my stomach, and my palms have grown clammy. My inner message board flashes word that I'm no longer in control of things; that a powerful outside

61

source has grabbed hold of my world. Suddenly I'm afraid—afraid for myself, afraid for my loved ones, afraid of the future.

The summer I turned 14, I spent several weeks at a church youth camp. I was away from home for the first time, and I fell in love with the nearby lake where campers gathered every afternoon. A persistent counselor tried to teach me a few basic strokes. I wasn't a good learner, but one afternoon I made up my mind to practice what I'd been taught. I leaped into deep water and tried to coordinate my arm and leg movements to stay afloat. Land seemed miles away and I had more doubts about my ability to handle the situation than I'd ever felt before. Again and again I dropped my leg in search of terra firma. My strength was almost gone before I felt the soft clay under my toes and sank exhausted in the shallows. Thirty years later, I can recall my horror at being unable to touch bottom.

Isn't that how we feel when the problems of life overwhelm our consciousness? We yearn for the security of firm ground, and when it isn't there we feel insecure. Many Christians are relieved to find that others share emotions of terror and anxiety when disaster strikes. Our bodies and minds seem to be equipped with defense mechanisms that send warning signals when confronted by danger. When these mechanisms go into action, they let us know that something we can't handle by ourselves lies just ahead. There's no need to feel guilty about our natural fears and insecurities. They aren't sinful; in fact, they should point the believer to God.

Isn't that the point of this event on the Sea of Galilee? The Lord Jesus wants His people to know that when they face adversity, they may receive help from Him.

Faith

It would make a neat climax to report that the disciples knelt in reverence and said to Jesus, "We fear the elements;

nevertheless, we recognize that You are the Son of God, Lord of whatever circumstances touch our lives. In complete confidence we claim Your divine authority over the wind and waves." Instead they shrieked, "Master, we are sinking! Do you not care?" (Mark 4:38). Their words blended tones of anger and terror.

We could wish for evidence of at least a little faith; however, the disciples were moving in the right direction. We make progress in handling the storms of life when we cry out to Jesus for help, even if our request isn't a textbook example of how to pray. As we acknowledge our dependence on the Lord and grow in our ability to cry for His help, we shall discover His perfect adequacy for our needs.

I appreciate the story about a little boy who was trying to carry a heavy rock to the opposite side of the yard. He would stagger a few steps, drop his load, then pick it up once more. It was obvious to his father, standing nearby, that the little fellow would never be able to maneuver the boulder to its destination. The father shouted, "Use all your strength, son, use all your strength." Dad was still urging the boy on when the fellow dropped his load for the last time.

"I am using all my strength," he shot back at his father.

"But you haven't asked for my help," replied the dad. We never employ all the resources available to us until we ask the Lord to help us. That's what the disciples demonstrated during their stormy night on the lake. We do well to follow their example. The Master is interested in the smallest details of daily living that pose problems for us and our loved ones.

The disciples were in no mood to contemplate their circumstances at the height of the gale, but perhaps later they were able to reflect on these events. Did they remember how Jesus had said, "'Let us cross over to the other side of the lake'" before they embarked? The fact that He promised safe arrival on the opposite shore should have given them con-

63

fidence. The realization that He was with them in the vessel should have stilled their anxieties. The One who makes promises and assures us of His presence has everything under control.

Such assurance brought calm to Becki Conway when the pretty teenager found herself in one of those sudden storms. Becki first noticed problems with her left knee during eighth grade cheerleading. A doctor assumed that tendons were being strained during a fast growth period. "She'll outgrow it," he declared.

When the problem persisted, other physicians were called in. They located a benign growth within the bone wall—something to watch. A year later, the biopsy showed a growing tumor. Many labs checked samples of the biopsy, then the family doctor made his decision. The leg would have to be amputated.

The Conway family was stunned by the news, but Becki accepted the situation better than her parents. Everyone was amazed that she felt no bitterness or depression, but quickly came to grips with reality.

How?

"I knew my God," Becki said confidently. "I had been saved as a child, and had given God my life. He was my friend, and I knew He wasn't going to let this experience be wasted."[1] Several years have passed since Becki's operation, and she still demonstrates remarkable faith in God's control.

Becki Conway's attitude comes to mind whenever I read the account of the storm and Jesus' action. In relating the incident, Mark twice uses the adjective "great." He speaks of the "great storm," then he adds that after Jesus spoke, there was a "great calm" (KJV). Becki reminds us that He may not immediately calm the storm around us, but we may count on Him to calm the storm within us. That's the calm we need more than any other.

Knowing that the Christ who loves us is Lord of our circumstances, we may shout to the world:

> *Whether the wrath of the storm-tossed sea,*
> *Or demons, or men, or whatever it be,*
> *No water can swallow the ship where lies*
> *The Master of ocean and earth and skies.*
> *"They all shall sweetly obey My will;*
> *Peace, be still! Peace, be still!"*[2]

My Personal Encounter with Jesus

Take a few minutes to ponder "sudden" happenings that could cause you to be afraid. What facts about Jesus Christ could you depend upon in such an emergency? How might His help become available to you? Memorize a Bible promise such as Rom. 8:28 or Isa. 43:1-2, verses that offer assurance of God's care in the storms of life.

My Prayer

Lord, I find it easy to identify with the disciples in the storm. Like them, I've been terrified by unexpected calamities that have pounded my life. From now on help me to remember that You are the Master of every circumstance, and give me confidence to claim Your authority over whatever threatens to engulf me. Amen.

Luke 8:26-39*
(cf. Matt. 8:28-34; Mark 5:1-20)

8

Cease-Fire for a Walking Civil War

During Jesus' stay in Galilee, critics buzzed around Him like heat-crazed gnats. They took exception to the way He trampled on their traditions, and they attacked His kind attitude toward notorious sinners. Yet there was one charge no one dared make against the Nazarene. Nobody ever accused Him of having a dull ministry.

Excitement and an aura of expectancy swirled around Jesus, and people learned that the unexpected might occur at any moment. His movements through the towns and villages of Galilee would have made an award-winning pilot film for a TV series.

Luke, the historian, takes us inside one of those action-packed days. First, Jesus encounters a fierce storm (Luke 8:22-25). No sooner had He calmed the lake in its turmoil, allowing the vessel to reach land, than He met a person in turmoil (vv. 26-39). Both incidents gave the Lord a platform to demonstrate His power over forces that no mere human could control.

66

The small boat carrying Jesus touched shore in the country of the Gadarenes, where the Syrian hills slope to the sea. Hardly had Jesus left the vessel when a crazed man who had terrorized the region for years dashed up and flung himself to the ground. Luke reports, "For a long time he had neither worn clothes nor lived in a house, but stayed among the tombs" (8:27).

What Jesus did for this pathetic individual demonstrates what He is able to accomplish in the person who is fragmented within and torn by discord. Several details of the story deserve emphasis.

Confusion

What a scene of confusion confronted Jesus! The deranged man's biographical sketch in the Gospels reads like data on someone who has tripped on acid once too often. According to Luke, the man lived in the tombs, far removed from civilized society. Mark adds, "He had often been fettered and chained up, but he had snapped his chains and broken the fetters. No one was strong enough to master him" (5:4). He cut himself on sharp stones, and from time to time the man's ear-splitting screams echoed through caves that dotted the rocky coast, striking fear into all who heard him.

In Matthew's version, travelers were careful to avoid the area inhabited by the deranged man. He comes across the page as a lonely, violent individual with suicidal tendencies.

And behind the man's fragmented personality were evil spirits who tramped through his feverish mind like a regiment of Roman soldiers.

This man in turmoil is a reminder of fragmented men and women who live in your town and mine. They seem to be always driven by conflicting values, influenced by forces outside of themselves. One young man, feeling himself inwardly pulled in many opposing directions, told a counselor, "I feel like a walking civil war."

Instead of being whole, healthy personalities, these individuals are marked by distorted priorities, about who they are and the real meaning of life. Their tragic approach to living recalls a line by British poet John Masefield about "broken things too broke to mend." Such brokenness and inward confusion would be familiar to Jesus. He faced these problems in the person of the demon-possessed man of Gadara.

Compassion

This incident also instructs us in the compassion that Jesus shows to confused, fragmented people. While others were avoiding the man, or trying to restrain him with chains, Jesus listened and gave the man His full attention. That in itself is a gift beyond price.

Dr. James Kennedy remarks that talking to some people is like talking to a lighthouse. "The beam of their attention focuses on you briefly and then flashes away in wide circles. A little later it comes back and hits you again, 'Hi! How are things in there?' But then the beam is gone again. . . . They never seem to bring all of their wits to bear upon the individual with whom they are talking."[1]

Jesus was different. He gave full attention to those he encountered in the days of His flesh. He still does. It's one evidence of the compassion He shows men and women who need a touch from Him.

If you look at the incident in a Bible where Jesus' words are printed in red, you notice how little the Lord actually said to the demoniac. The emphasis was not on verbal communication but presence. The fact that Jesus was there, giving full attention, showing concern, was the chief evidence of His compassion.

68

When Jesus did speak, He asked the man to give his name. Was the Master's attitude like the kindly concern of an adult who intercepts an obviously lost boy or girl? "What is your name?" asks the friend. The question, voiced in a calm, reassuring tone, stops the flow of tears and opens the way for communication to take place. In a similar way, Jesus radiated coolness and compassion by what He was and by what He said and did. He bid the evil spirits to leave the man, setting the stage for a further development in the story.

Change

Notice the change that occurs in the demoniac. What a "before and after" scene could be painted by the artist who compares Luke 8:27-28 with verse 35. When townspeople rushed to the shoreline to see what had happened, they "found the man from whom the devils had gone out sitting at his feet clothed and in his right mind" (v. 35).

Jesus wanted to prove to the man that the demons were indeed gone, so He allowed them to enter a herd of pigs. In that region the hills extend rapidly to the water, and the pigs rushed headlong to their doom. Now Jesus and the disciples could say, "Look, friend, you've been set free." There was visible evidence that the previously fragmented personality was now whole. A remarkable change had taken place, thanks to the presence and word of the Master.

Throughout history, individuals of renown have looked in vain for ways to change human nature for the better. One person may espouse a political formula, while someone else may suggest an economic or social program designed to improve the lot of mankind. While certain efforts prove moderately successful in bettering outward conditions, the inner nature of individuals remains a problem.

Karl Marx recognized the limitations of systems when he declared, "Philosophers have only interpreted the world in various ways; the point is to change it." You may read Marx's remark on his tomb in London's Highgate Cemetery.

In contrast to the would-be change agents of history, Jesus brings dramatic transformations that are both deep-seated and lasting. He offers the promise of wholeness to persons who languish in varied stages of personality disintegration. He invites men and women to let Him bring change, and history shows that He makes changes that are fundamental, changes that affect whole societies.

The year was 1956. In early January, five American missionaries were brutally murdered on a riverbank in Ecuador by stone-age savages who resisted the Christians' attempts to bring them the gospel. Time passed and a few of the Auca tribespeople allowed Bible translators to infiltrate the group. At last a small group of believers formed a church and built a thatched-roof structure for worship. Some of the killers received Christ as Savior and lent their support to the translation of the Scriptures into their dialect.

Nine years later, Don Johnson, director of Wycliffe Bible Translators in Ecuador, flew into Aucaland with the first printed copies of the Gospel of Mark in Auca. The new Scriptures were to be dedicated in an Easter service.

"The service started with a hymn chant led by Dyuwi, one of the five killers, and the chorister of the church. His hymn book has three hymns, two of which he wrote himself.

"Dyuwi stood again and led about twenty children in singing 'Jesus Loves Me' in the Auca language." Then Aucas, including some who had participated in the killing of the missionaries, took turns reciting verses they had learned. A man named Kimo closed the Easter service with prayer, practically preaching a sermon for 15 minutes.

Johnson closed his description of the service by adding: "Less than ten years ago this was dangerous territory, controlled completely by killers. Now other groups of Indians are

70

moving into the territory which was once controlled by their arch-enemies. The Gospel changes the personal lives of individuals and that in turn makes a sociological change in the country. The Auca Easter service is living proof that the Gospel has power to change people from savages to Christians."[2]

Jesus meets the confusion of a fragmented personality with compassion, then He offers to change it so that it no longer expresses itself in destructive ways.

Charge

The final stage in the encounter is the charge Jesus gives to the man. Since the demoniac, now healed and in his right mind, wanted to follow Jesus, it seems surprising to read of the Master's refusal. "'Go back home,' he said, 'and tell them everything that God has done for you.' The man went all over the town spreading the news of what Jesus had done for him" (Luke 8:39).

The Lord probably followed this strategy for two reasons. First, the experience would glow with reality to the man every time he told his story. Part of his therapy was the constant recitation of details about the compassionate Teacher who calmed troubled hearts.

Jesus may have had another purpose in mind. According to the account in Mark, the man was to go, not only to the closest village, but also to Decapolis, 10 cities populated by nearly a million people. Most residents were Gentiles, and the evangelistic ministry of the ex-demoniac would make them aware of the Lord, many for the first time.

The man obeyed and "published" (KJV)—the Greek word for heralding or preaching—the story of his encounter with Jesus.

The reasons behind Jesus' charge to the man of Gadara are similar to the reasons for His commission to changed men

71

and women of every age. The telling of our personal testimony helps us to relive the excitement of that earlier meeting with the Lord and reinforces our confidence in the reality of Christ's power. Moreover, as we share this encounter with unsaved men and women, some of them learn for the first time about the significant changes the Lord Jesus can make in one's life.

Many years ago the historian Kenneth Scott Latourette showed that the greatest gains made by the Church took place during her second and third generations. Persecution and peril were rife, yet during this period of sweeping advance there is no evidence of any conspicuous leader. No key evangelist or theologian guided God's people to their triumphs. In other words, the Church moved forward on the witness of rank and file members. Obscure, dedicated, changed, these men and women shared Christ, and He blessed their witness with increased numbers who trusted Him as their Savior and Lord.

Where do you fit in the picture? If you feel like a "walking civil war," you need to know that Jesus Christ is still a compassionate, powerful Savior. He stands ready to change your life. But you must also know that with the change He asks you to be His witness. His message is still, "Go home and tell what wonderful things I have done for you."

My Personal Encounter with Jesus

Do you need the quieting touch of Christ at some specific point in your own life? Or do you need to spread the news about His power, based on what He has demonstrated in your experience? If there is inner conflict within, ask the Lord to bring healing to your spirit, then seek His help in telling others of His power to make men and women whole.

My Prayer

Lord, sometimes I become so aware of the turmoil in my life that I forget Your power to bring inner healing. And on other occasions I forget that I'm to be a witness of Your power in the world. Touch my life at the points where I need to be made whole, then touch my lips and enable me to share Your wonderful works with a world in desperate need. Amen.

9

Trading First Impressions
for a Lasting Gift

During the last few years I've noticed something about first impressions. They aren't entirely accurate. In fact, our final verdict on an individual may be totally different from the feelings we had after meeting that person for the first time.

In one of my churches my first meeting with the treasurer made me uneasy. When she introduced herself, her piercing eyes penetrated the emotional shield I was hiding behind until I knew the members better. Right away, my early warning system flashed an alert. I urged my wife to beware of the treasurer, for I was certain she would be the first person in the power structure to threaten my leadership. Six years later I traveled over 1,000 miles to conduct her funeral. I wept, knowing that I had lost my closest supporter and one of the dearest friends a pastor's family could hope to find. My earliest impression was light-years removed from reality.

In the same church I gave pastoral care to a woman in her 60s who was frequently confined to the hospital for assorted illnesses. We became fast friends, and one afternoon she shared a memory of my first Sunday morning service. I was midway through the sermon when she had turned to a friend and whispered, "Where on earth did they find him?" I was glad she waited until we knew each other better before she revealed her feelings.

First Impressions of Jesus

We all form first impressions about neighbors, people at work, and the folks we meet at church. That's human nature. In the days when Jesus ministered here on earth, men and women quickly advanced first opinions about Him, but sometimes their initial verdict wasn't the one they finally adopted. The Master's encounter with a Samaritan woman is a case in point.

The story really begins in Judea where Jesus achieved fame during several months of teaching and healing. His followers were now baptizing more people than had John the Baptist, causing Jewish authorities to intensify their interest in the Galilean.

In fact, the authorities grew so interested that Jesus decided to close His work in Judea and return to Galilee. Some day in the future He would meet the jealous wrath of the Pharisees head-on. For now He had a teaching mission to fulfill.

In Jesus' day, Palestine was divided into three distinct areas. To the south lay Judea, small in territory but boasting the important city of Jerusalem. Galilee was the northern province, and even though many Jews lived there, the region was considered Gentile turf. Sandwiched between north and south lay Samaria. Samaritans and Jews hated each other, but the fastest route to Galilee led through Samaria, so Jesus and His disciples moved in that direction. At noon they arrived at a well dug nearly 2,000 years before by Jacob. Jesus rested there while the disciples walked into a nearby village to buy food.

While they were away, a woman approached the well to draw water. She wasn't expecting the stranger who sat there; in fact, she usually planned this errand for the hottest time of day to avoid people. She hated their stares, their snide remarks, and the names they attached to her "liberated" lifestyle.

Her annoyance grew when the stranger asked for a drink. He was obviously a Jew, one of the hated "them" she had heard about since childhood. His clothing and accent gave Him away, and the Samaritan woman's mind flashed reasons to buttress her feelings.

More than 700 years earlier, Samaria had been overrun by the armies of Assyria. Foreigners who worshipped idols were imported, and many of them married those who paid lip service to the God of Israel. New religions had sprung up, replacing the old doctrines and restrictions of the Jewish religion. Later, residents of Jerusalem had refused to allow Samaritans to assist in rebuilding the capital city, causing further schism between the groups. By the time of this encounter by Jacob's well, "Samaritan" was little more than an obscenity used by Jews, while both sides treated each other with contempt.

But Jesus asked the woman for a drink.

"'What!'" she exclaimed. "'You, a Jew, ask a drink of me, a Samaritan woman?'" (John 4:9). She quickly added that Jews and Samaritans never used a common drinking vessel, and only one bucket was available.

Jesus responded, "'If only you knew ... who it is that is asking you for a drink, you would have asked him and he would have given you living water'" (v. 10).

"Living water." The woman understood the expression to mean spring water bubbling from the ground, in contrast to water that stood at the bottom of this well.

"'You have no bucket and this well is deep. How can you

give me "living water"?'" the woman asked (v. 11). She reasoned that if there had been running water in the neighborhood, someone as great as Jacob would have found it. If this well represented the patriarch's best effort, who did Jesus think he was to boast of living water? Her first impression, that Jesus was nothing more than an arrogant Jew, seemed to be confirmed by their conversation.

But Jesus persisted. At last the woman said, "'Sir . . . give me that water, and then I shall not be thirsty, nor have to come all this way to draw'" (v. 15).

"'Go home, call your husband and come back,'" responded Jesus (v. 16).

When the woman answered, "'I have no husband,'" Jesus countered, "'You are right, . . . in saying that you have no husband, for, although you have had five husbands, the man with whom you are now living is not your husband'" (vv. 17-18).

"'Sir,' she replied, 'I can see that you are a prophet'" (v. 19). Her opinion of Jesus is changing. He must be a representative of God to know the intimate details of her life.

Their conversation continues until the woman says, "'I know that Messiah' (that is Christ) 'is coming. When he comes he will tell us everything.' Jesus said, 'I am he, I who am speaking to you now'" (vv. 25-26).

When she heard that, the woman returned to the village to tell people, "'Come and see a man who has told me everything I ever did. Could this be the Messiah?'" (vv. 28-29). She was so intent on spreading the news that she left her waterpot beside the well.

Does the Samaritan woman remind you of anyone in your circle of influence? Maybe she's like your neighbor whose first impression of Jesus is tied to history. Such a person believes that He lived and died like any other figure from the past, no more, no less. Perhaps His system of ethics deserves a closer look, but there's nothing particularly attractive about Jesus the Man.

The Samaritan woman's past experience with Jews effectively blocked her view of Jesus. She could only see Him in relation to things she had heard and people she had met, so her first impression wasn't adequate. She needed to know the real Christ.

Reality with Jesus

Once the woman began to interact with Jesus, several trends began to emerge. These trends are worth examining, because when people today really see Christ in our lives, or by serious study of Scripture, reality will break through as it did to the Samaritan.

First, people have deep-seated spiritual needs that they manage to keep hidden from view. In moments of honesty, men and women are forced to admit the existence of those needs, to themselves and to others.

The Samaritan woman seems to have her life together when she first meets Jesus, but soon her yearning for "living water" breaks through the sham. And the longer she talks with Jesus, the more she exposes her inner thirst. It becomes apparent that she not only wants physical water, but her spirit craves the kind of satisfaction that only God is able to give.

When I see people in my community living for momentary pleasures or plunging into the latest religious fad, I think of the sinkholes that appear in sunbelt states following efforts to find oil or water. Holes in the ground become visible after drilling has occurred, but nobody can fill them. Pour tons of dirt and gravel into the holes, but the hole will still be there tomorrow morning. Life is like that when we are out of touch with God. Emotionally and intellectually we try to plug the sinkhole of the spirit, but nothing works. That's what happened to the woman in our story. Apparently she was trying to fill the emptiness in her spirit with sexual adventures, but in the presence of Jesus she was forced to admit that she needed something else to bring lasting satisfaction.

Behind every facade lies a human spirit that can only be filled by a personal relationship with Jesus Christ. He alone is able to satisfy the thirsty soul with living water, that perpetual source of life.

A *second* truth comes through this encounter between Jesus and the Samaritan woman. Like her, I only see myself as a sinner when I stand in the presence of Christ. Adultery didn't appear so bad until Christ described her wayward activities. On His lips, her sin loomed large as life, and she quickly changed the subject to something less threatening.

I've had a few experiences that made me aware of reality in contrast to fantasies I'd accepted as truth. One of the most memorable took place the summer I turned 11. I read several books by expert checker players, then applied what I'd learned against kids in my neighborhood. My studies paid off and I was practically unbeatable—until a man up the street challenged me to a test of skills.

Twenty years earlier, George had been state checker champion, but I psyched myself into thinking that his game had grown rusty. I was sure that he'd prove vulnerable to some of the moves described in the books.

He wasn't.

After I'd been wiped out in game after game, I began to see George's strategy. In effect he was letting me tie a rope around my own neck, then he would jerk the noose tight with a succession of brilliant double and triple jumps. After that evening, I didn't care to see a checkerboard, ever. The presence of a master brought my limited talents into sharp focus.

Take another example. Nowadays my major interest is teaching the Bible. Every week I spend many hours preparing sermons and studies designed to bring out the beauty and meaning of God's Word. Thanks to good training and a large library of study aids I'm able to prepare messages that many listeners tell me are helpful. Sometimes I feel good about my performance; I sense that I've given people high-quality work.

However, what I do pales when I listen to the truly great expositors of Scripture. The Sunday after I've heard John Stott, Sidlow Baxter, or Paul Rees, I have no struggle to achieve humility. No matter how kind the compliments of my congregation, I know that my performance is far below that of the expositor I've heard during the week. The distance between us is obvious.

Did the Samaritan woman feel like that as she talked with Jesus and recognized His purity, His love, His relationship with the Father? Something like that occurs when our friends who seem to have little spiritual interest come into personal contact with Christ. They may observe Him at work in our lives, or they may be part of a Bible study, but the effect is usually the same. They recognize themselves to be sinners as they note the sharp contrast between their standards and His holiness.

A *third* truth I find in this account is that, like the woman at the well, we may receive a gift that satisfies our craving for spiritual reality, while at the same time cancelling our guilt and sin.

Jesus used the figure of living water to describe forgiveness and eternal life. He talked about bestowing this "water" as a gift, the only requirement being acceptance by each recipient. There are several hints that the Samaritan woman received the gift Jesus offered her at the well.

We notice that she became so excited that she left her waterpot and dashed into the city to share the news about Christ with townspeople. Before long, a large crowd gathered to meet Jesus for themselves. Many of the people believed in Him because of the woman's testimony.

She had a need in her spirit, and Jesus helped her to face it.

She needed to see herself as God saw her, so Jesus held her life against the purity of His own person.

She wanted a gift that would cancel the penalty of her sin and satisfy her yearning for reality; Jesus offered her "living water."

Aren't you glad that first impressions can change?

Especially when that change helps us experience Jesus as He really is.

My Personal Encounter with Jesus

How has your impression of Jesus changed since you first thought seriously about Him? Does He want you to see Him as more powerful, more loving, more in control than you have recently perceived Him to be? Does His patience in revealing himself to the Samaritan woman make you feel uneasy? hopeful? What step will you take next in order to know Him better?

My Prayer

Lord, I'm afraid that I've been content to depend too much on my first impression of You. Lead me along toward a better understanding of who You are, and what You can do through me in the world. And make me as excited about the discoveries I make as the Samaritan woman was about her encounter with You. Amen.

10

The Care and Handling of a Failure

Failure is everyone's acquaintance, but nobody's friend. One day it drops into life suddenly like an uninvited guest, another time it shadows every move whether we're at home or on the job. An unknown writer observed that it takes some people all their lives to become failures, while others achieve it in just a few years. Since all of us will come eyeball to eyeball with a major failure sometime, we need to learn all we can about this adversary. Where shall we look for information and for a workable strategy to handle failure in our lives?

Let's start by defining our foe. According to a dictionary, failure means to fall short of success in something expected or approved. That's good for an opener, but it still doesn't explain how to cope when failure strikes. We need something more.

How about studying the feelings that engulf us when we fail? Choose the word that best describes your emotions right after you've flubbed it at work or fallen short of the high standards you've set for personal affairs. Would your word be *anger? despair? depression? withdrawal?* Looking within may help a person to understand what's happening, but this information doesn't guarantee that an individual will then handle failure well. Isn't there more?

Christians believe that their best help comes from the Bible, a Who's Who of people who "fell short of success." The Record includes men and women, rich and poor, the famous and unknowns. You won't find any cover-ups in the Bible. Here's one place where failure is portrayed just as it happened. But every account of failure is framed in encouragement. Scripture shows how God treats those who fail and how He aids people who yearn to rise above their mistakes.

Peter Aided by Christ

Speaking of failures in the Bible, Simon Peter belongs in a class by himself. The blustering fisherman seems always to be saying the wrong words, exhibiting the wrong emotions, rushing headlong into the wrong actions. Let's bring one of Peter's failures under the microscope.

On a sun-drenched morning in Galilee, Peter is mending his fishing nets along the shore. The previous night he and his companions had spent hours trying for a big catch. All their professional skills had been brought into play—the right place, the right equipment, the right methods. According to experts, Peter should have brought in enough fish to feed half the town; but, in his own words, "'We were hard at work all night and caught nothing at all'" (Luke 5:5). Shed a tear for Peter; he failed in an area where we would expect him to succeed. So much for the details. Now let us observe how the Lord treats him at this embarrassing moment, for His reaction will show the kind of treatment we may expect when we, like Peter, fail at something important.

Failures Need to Know

First, Jesus wants those who fail to know something. He wants us to know that we aren't rejected, but that He comes to us in the hour of failure to comfort and offer help. If you want to see this principle at work in Peter's life, underline some of the action clauses in Luke 5:1-4: "He stood" . . . "the people crowded" . . . "He noticed two boats" . . . "He got into one of the boats" . . . "He went on teaching" . . . "He said to Simon." We catch a glimpse of Jesus instructing a crowd of eager listeners, but then He notices the man who had failed and moves toward him. Jesus speaks to Peter and finally dismisses the multitude so He may deal with the fisherman alone.

Isn't it incredible that Jesus would take valuable time away from teaching the crowd to deal with one defeated fisherman? Peter didn't look like the type of person who could further the Galilean's career or extend His influence in the region. It's striking to read how many times the Lord reached out to such individuals. He was constantly helping unlikely, unlovely men and women who had failed in the midst of life.

I'm glad that Jesus moved toward failures, because I can assure people that He still acts that way toward those who have messed up their lives in some disturbing ways.

One year, right after Christmas, I received a penciled note from a man in Gary, Ind. The writer had served time in prison and apparently was having a tough time adjusting to his new freedom. He told me that he had wandered into the bus depot on Christmas Eve, and someone had given him a gospel tract I'd written a couple of years before. My name and address was printed on the leaflet, so the man decided to ask for my help. He wasn't looking for money, only for answers. He wondered if "a guy must have a perfect record with God in order to become a Christian"? The ex-con might have added, "If one's life has to be spotless before God will take an interest in him, forget it!"

As I thought about how to reply, I remembered Peter and how the Lord Jesus made a special effort to touch the fisherman's life. I never heard from the man again, but I like to think that he made the same discovery as Peter on the shores of Galilee. The Lord is vitally concerned about men and women who have less than perfect records.

In the days of the great sailing vessels, the signal flags BNC meant, "I will not abandon you." This was the most important promise a ship could make as it drew alongside a distressed sister. Here was help, encouragement, the promise that a friend was near. "I will not abandon you"—that's the message Jesus Christ sends to people who need His love. He seeks us despite our failures. We can count on that fact, for it's something He wants us to know.

Failures Need to See

This incident also indicates that Jesus wants those who fail to see something. In effect He wants us to see two things—our present selves and our potential selves.

Peter got a good look at himself when the Lord performed the miracle and caused swarms of fish to enter the nets. Authorities point out that since this event took place early in Jesus' ministry, it may have been Peter's first ringside seat at a genuine miracle. He was overwhelmed by the power and perfections of Christ, but he also saw himself. Perhaps that explains why he cried out, "Go, Lord, leave me, sinner that I am!'" (Luke 5:8). Weaknesses, limitations, failures—Peter saw all of these human qualities, and he didn't care for the view. He knew that his present life made him unworthy of the Lord's presence.

Jesus didn't answer the fisherman's sudden prayer, for He saw that Peter had already learned the all-important lesson.

Peter now understood that he couldn't cope with life on his own terms and in his own strength. When we grasp that same truth, we stand at the threshold of a miracle. Those who admit failure and cast themselves upon the grace of God are moving in the direction Jesus intends for us to take.

The Lord wants us to behold our potential once we see what we are in the present. In answer to Peter's plea, the Master replied, "'Do not be afraid . . . from now on you will be catching men'" (Luke 5:10).

During an earlier meeting with the rugged fisherman, the Master had called attention to Peter's potential value for the Kingdom. "Thou art . . . thou shalt be" was the way Jesus put it (John 1:42, KJV), a coupling of the actual and the possible. A hot, hasty nature for the present, but a potential for spiritual power that would shake the world—this is what Jesus saw in the fisherman. Christ can take our possibilities and convert them into actualities. By His grace we may become what we ought to be.

Again and again in Scripture we see the Lord pointing to potential in a man or woman and bringing out that hidden strength in the crucible of daily affairs. One thinks of Gideon, hiding from the Midianites, yet seen by God as the potential deliverer of his people. Surrendered to God, that potential was transformed into reality.

Moses, retired from active duty, was appointed to lead the children of Israel out of bondage in Egypt. God saw potential even after Moses had apparently given up hope of special usefulness to either God or man. Do you hear Him saying to you, "Don't be afraid, there's something I'd like to make of your life"?

The governor of Washington was asked to host a visiting evangelist who was holding a crusade in the capital city of Olympia. The governor, a widely respected Christian, knew about the evangelist's remarkable achievements but had never met the man prior to the meetings. He expected that the preacher would be tall, handsome, a dynamic specimen of the gospel he proclaimed. Instead the governor came home to find his guest was none of the above. His face must have betrayed disappointment, for the evangelist smiled and said, "Governor, isn't it wonderful what God can use!"

It was and it is (just ask Peter). The Lord wants us to see what He is able to do in our lives, even when we've failed. He wants us to see that eventual success is possible with His resources applied to our weakness.

Failures Need to Do

Let's dip once more into the account in Luke's Gospel. This time we notice that Jesus wants those who have failed to do something. The loser in life is to call Jesus "Lord" (5:8) and to echo Peter's response, "At thy word I will" (v. 5, KJV).

The Christian has the wonderful privilege of calling upon One who is beyond that person's self. As the believer submits to Him as Lord and allows Him to produce His supernatural strength and power, Paul's words flash with meaning—"I can do all things through Christ which strengtheneth me" (Phil. 4:13, KJV).

Many men and women stare failure in the face and say to themselves, "I'll never try again." Perhaps Peter felt that way, too, but almost before he realized what was happening, Jesus was at his side telling him to try again; to go back to the place where he had failed and put down the nets one more time. There was an important difference from the night before. This time Jesus was in the vessel and He was issuing the instructions.

When the Lord gives you a promise from His Word, you may act upon it with confidence. Jesus says, "Make Me your Lord in these circumstances," and as you take that step, you may know that He never fails.

In this chapter Jesus teaches that failure need not be final. Despite previous blunders in our lives, He seeks us, helping us see what we have the potential to become by His grace. He encourages us to go back to the scene of past failures and try again—with Him in control.

Out of the past comes the story of a Scottish minister named John Robertson. He was defeated in the ministry. The glow had faded from his soul, power drained from his preaching, and he determined to leave the church. Before writing a letter to his superiors, Robertson went into the pulpit and knelt to pray.

"O God," he intoned, "40 years ago Thou didst commission me to preach, but I have blundered and failed, and I want to resign this morning." As he prayed, the brokenness and penitence of his soul shook him.

The sob of his heart was hushed, however, as he heard a voice within replying, "John Robertson, 'tis true I commissioned you 40 years ago; 'tis true you have blundered and failed; but, John Robertson, I am not here for you to resign your commission. I am here to re-sign your commission." As a result of that encounter, the man of God entered upon the most helpful, fruitful phase of his long ministry.

Again and again, I have heard the Voice that brought encouragement to John Robertson. On Sunday afternoons when I recall a less-than-satisfactory preaching effort, and late at night as I muse on mistakes in judgment, missed opportunities, and impatience with members of my family, I'm tempted to nudge the old fisherman. I want to say, "Move over, Peter; make room for one more person who needs to say, 'Depart from me; for I am a sinful man, O Lord'" (Luke 5:8, KJV).

But just before I quit, there's that Voice—"I am here to re-sign your commission."

In the quietness of my spirit I whisper back, "Thanks, Lord. Yes, I'll give it another shot—as long as You guide me and supply strength."

Now, where are those fish?

My Personal Encounter with Jesus

Where have I failed recently? At work? In my home? In my own inner life? Wait quietly before the Lord until He reminds you of a specific experience.

Now Jesus is saying, "Let's do it again." What new approach does He suggest? What is He asking of you? Picture yourself making another attempt with Jesus by your side. How does it feel?

My Prayer

Lord, when I yearn for a life without hardships and mistakes, remind me that oaks grow strong in contrary winds; that diamonds are fashioned under intense pressure. Help me to remember that failure is an opportunity to grow, and not a total disaster. Lead me forward from defeat with new trust in Your power. Amen.

11

Measured Steps from Doubt to Faith

Roy Riegels and Thomas, the disciple of Jesus, both deserve better treatment from the history books, for these men are usually remembered only because of mistakes that made them look like losers. Actually they should be recognized as winners, for they rebounded from failure to achieve great successes. Other people have been acclaimed as heroes for accomplishing far less.

Every sports fan has heard about Riegels' boner. He was the starting center for the University of California, playing in the 1929 Rose Bowl game, when he made one of the most famous mistakes in football history. Midway through the second quarter, Georgia Tech fumbled on their own 25-yard line, and Riegels scooped up the loose ball. For reasons still unclear, the Bears' captain-elect took off toward *his own* goal. He had covered nearly 75 yards and was within a foot of the goal line when a teammate caught his attention and turned him around. It was too late, as a Tech tackler dropped the stunned ball carrier in the shadow of his team's end zone. A punt was blocked, causing a safety—the difference in the final score. Tech won 8-7, and Riegels' wrong-way gallop was chiseled in the record books forever.

The following season, Riegels was named to the all-conference squad and was mentioned in several all-American selections by nationally known sportswriters. In later years he became an award-winning insurance salesman, selling over $1 million worth of coverage annually; but when people mention Roy Riegels, they discuss only his mistake one New Year's afternoon.

Thomas is another figure whose reputation suffers from a momentary lapse. Mention his name and someone is sure to remember "He's the disciple who insisted, '"Unless I see the mark of the nails on his hands, unless I put my finger into the place where the nails were, and my hand into his side, I will not believe"'" (John 20:25). It takes a sharp Bible student to recall that Thomas also made one of the loftiest confessions of Jesus to be found in Scripture, "'My Lord and my God!'" (v. 28). Tradition adds that Thomas carried the gospel to India where he died as a martyr for his faith in Christ. Thomas may have been a late starter, but he surged ahead of everyone else in recognizing that Jesus was really the Son of God.

Still, Thomas was a doubter. Why? What made it so difficult for him to accept the news of Christ's resurrection? For one thing, Thomas' personality shows a negative streak, and he seems to have been put together in the minor key. We see this side of Thomas when the Lord announced His intention to go to Bethany and touch Lazarus, despite the open hostility of Jewish leaders. Thomas replied, "'Let us also go, that we may die with him'" (John 11:16). That was Thomas, ready to go down with the sinking ship.

When his fears were finally realized and Jesus was crucified, Thomas was filled with despair and withdrew from the others. The reports about a risen Christ were not to be believed, whether the source was the women at the tomb (their eyes were probably full of tears so they couldn't see clearly; besides, they were overwrought by the experience they had just passed through), or the men who met Him in the Upper Room (sheer hallucination caused by frayed nerves and wishful thinking about what could never be; they wanted to see Jesus so badly they imagined they actually saw Him).

In our moments of honesty, most of us find it easy to identify with Thomas. Had we been living in those days, chances are we would have echoed his doubts about a living Christ who walked through locked doors, then suddenly disappeared. We know how Thomas felt because we have our own pockets of doubt, even though we claim to be sincere followers of the Lord. Denying that these feelings exist may bring temporary relief, but something more is needed to strengthen our confidence in the Christian faith. Right here, Thomas serves as a helpful model. As we examine his measured steps from "I will not believe" to "My Lord and my God!" we learn three principles for making the journey from doubt to faith.

Spell Out Doubts

Thomas talked about his inner feelings, about his mental reservations regarding a risen Christ. In expressing doubt, Thomas was in the minority among his fellow disciples, and his open attitude would keep him in the minority among Christians today. Believers who wrestle with serious doubts about their faith usually repress these feelings, perhaps fearing that they will be thought "unspiritual" by friends. The standards of society must shoulder the blame for a great deal of this hesitancy to reveal oneself.

Author Sidney Jourard likens most people in the Western world to players in a high-stakes game. He says, "In a poker game, no man discloses his hand to the other players. Instead, he tries to dissemble and bluff. . . . in a society which pits man against man, as in a poker game, people do keep a poker face; they wear a mask and let no one know what they are up to."

Jourard continues, "We are said to be a society dedicated, among other things, to the pursuit of truth. Yet, disclosure is often penalized."[1] Instead of accepting our feelings and spelling out doubts to Christian friends, we make believe that we are different, and in the process cut ourselves off from an important source of help.

While social patterns may keep some Christians from airing their doubts, a different muzzle inhibits other believers. These are conscientious men and women who fear that it's sinful to employ their minds in matters of faith. They have been taught to look on human reason with suspicion and to accept every pronouncement from the pulpit without asking questions.

Francis Schaeffer, one of the great thinkers in the contemporary Church, begs to differ. He insists, "It is not more spiritual to believe without asking questions. It is not more Biblical. It is less Biblical and eventually it will be less spiritual because the whole man will not be involved." Dr. Schaeffer agrees that those who come to Christ must come as small children, but he asks, "Did you ever see a little child who didn't ask questions?"[2] We are made for thinking as well as for feeling, and we deny part of our God-given personalities by failing to raise issues that trouble us.

Until a person works through doubts to faith in Christ, it is questionable whether that individual has made a true commitment. While using the right words and smiling at the right places in the service, such a person is only hitchhiking on someone else's relationship with the Lord, unless doubts have been dealt with.

Don't be afraid to spell out your doubts, for Christianity welcomes investigation. It is firmly grounded on time-space events that have been accurately recorded and faithfully preserved.

Josh McDowell, a popular apologist for the Christian faith, argues that becoming a Christian isn't like taking a blind leap into the dark. On the contrary such a commitment means exercising intelligent faith in Christ based on evidence presented in Scripture.

The pilot who never checks his aircraft—fuel supply, fluid levels, and pressures—before taking off isn't an example of faith. That's stupidity. Faith means running a series of performance tests and coming to a conclusion based on solid evidence. Then the pilot commits himself to the plane, based on his findings. In a similar way, a decision to follow Christ after examining the evidence is a commitment with meaning.

Do you have questions and doubts about spiritual matters? Don't bottle them up inside or make believe they don't exist, but spell them out to someone who will help you find answers. That was Thomas' first measured step toward faith.

Stay in Touch with Christian Friends

Danny grew up in church activities, in fact he was a Sunday School teacher's dream. He never presented discipline problems, not even in the roughest class of junior boys. Adults whispered that Danny would make an outstanding minister someday. After two quarters at the state university, Danny developed some doubts about those lessons and sermons from his childhood. That summer he dropped out of church and drifted away from his former Christian friends. Adults said it was a shame what a secular school could do to a young person, but nobody reached out to offer Danny friendship and understanding.

Maybe Thomas was moving in that direction after the death of Jesus; that would explain why he was absent when Jesus appeared to the other disciples that Easter evening. But the followers of Christ wouldn't let Thomas go. The New Testament records that they went after the doubter and said, "'We have seen the Lord'" (John 20:25). The original language shows that the disciples didn't visit Thomas once, but they went to him again and again, repeating their experience with the risen Lord. Their efforts paid off, for the following Sunday night Thomas showed up for the closed-door meeting. So did Jesus, confronting the doubter with the very pieces of evidence he had requested. Continuing contact between Thomas and the disciples helped to move the doubter to full faith in the Son of God.

A college student who received a mild dose of Christianity back home, but claimed to be an agnostic, took an active part in campus activities. On the outside he seemed to be one of the happiest students in the university, yet under the surface he felt unhappy and unfulfilled. To make matters worse, witnessing Christians in his dorm wouldn't leave him alone. They showed love in many small ways, but they also challenged the young man to be intellectually honest in facing the claims of Christ.

When he couldn't stand their persistence any longer, the student went all out to refute their faith. He studied the Bible's account of the Resurrection, prophecies of the Old Testament, and generally tried to refute the reliability of Scripture. In the end his evidence pointed in a single direction—the events and doctrines of the Bible were true. The student became a believer in Christ and has shared his discoveries with young people from coast to coast. Besides stressing the reliability of God's Word, he also emphasizes the importance of staying in touch with Christians, even when a person harbors doubts about the faith. "I was loved out of my agnosticism by caring Christians," he tells his listeners.

Study the Evidence

When Thomas finally came into contact with Jesus, risen from the tomb, the Master's attitude wasn't judgmental. He didn't cajole the doubting disciple in front of the others but simply presented solid evidence and invited Thomas to examine His claim. "'Reach your finger here; see my hands. Reach your hand here and put it into my side. Be unbelieving no longer, but believe'" (John 20:27). Will the Lord treat 20th-century doubters with less kindness than He demonstrated to Thomas?

Many outstanding scholars offer evidence for the reliability of the New Testament and consequently its high claims for the person of Christ. For example, the manuscripts from the first centuries after Christ have been remarkably preserved, compared with other writings. F. F. Bruce, a leading scholar from Manchester University, England, checked the New Testament documents against Caesar's *Gallic War* (composed about 50 B.C.). While only 9 or 10 good manuscripts exist of Caesar's work, the oldest being 900 years later than his day, there are at least 3,000 good Greek manuscripts of the New Testament. The earliest complete manuscript dates back to A.D. 350, while parts of the Gospels date less than 50 years after they were first written down. Dr. Bruce declares, "The evidence for our New Testament writings is ever so much greater than the evidence for many writings of classical authors, the authenticity of which no one dreams of questioning."[3]

A visit to most Christian bookstores will turn up an armful of printed and recorded materials that document the reliability of our historic Christian faith. Study the evidence, for if Christianity is historically accurate, it will stand firm in the marketplace of ideas.

We need to keep in mind that some people may have all their intellectual objections answered, yet still refuse to trust Christ and embrace the faith. That's because these "objections" are only a smokescreen for a different kind of problem, one involving the will. In reality, such individuals don't care whether the Gospel accounts ring true, they insist on retaining full authority over their lives and will reject Christ no matter how the evidence falls. More people may be kept out of the kingdom of God by cold feet than by cold logic. It takes the Spirit of God to bring conviction, not just human efforts to resolve intellectual doubts about Christianity.

But if your problem is really about doubts—*honest* doubts about Jesus Christ and His claims—walk in the steps of Thomas. Spell out your doubts to an individual or group of Christians who will accept you as you are, but who will help you work through the issues you find it hard to accept; stay in contact with Christian friends, and don't turn away from the kinds of settings where Christ himself may be waiting to communicate reality; and study the evidence put forth by scholars who are giving their lives to show that Christianity is truth.

Pity Roy Riegels. We can't rewrite his wrong-way dash in the Rose Bowl, but we can follow Thomas in his shift from doubt to faith. Just because he doubted, we have no reason to live in the shadows. We owe him a debt of gratitude for raising these questions and for showing us how to move into the sunlight of a vibrant Christian faith.

My Personal Encounter with Jesus

What are some of the doubts you feel from time to time? What are some of the questions you wish you could put to Christ, personally? Consider some steps you might take to find satisfying answers to these questions. Could a friend help you make progress toward the solutions? What step will you take next?

My Prayer

Lord, despite the many evidences of Your work that I've seen for myself, I still have down times when I wonder if it's real. Help me to identify my doubts and face them honestly, but remind me that my problem may be due to cold feet, not cold logic. Above all, I'm thankful that You don't quit on me when I raise these questions. Open my eyes to the answers You want me to find. Amen.

12

Washbasins and Bent Knees

Good . . . better . . . best.

Advertisers use these terms to describe the relative merits of a product line, but the words may also be applied to three forms of communication. To *hear* a message is good, to *see* a message is better, but to both *hear and see* a message is best of all. We find an example of "best" communication in Jesus' encounter with His disciples in the Upper Room.

The Upper Room, where Jesus and the Twelve celebrated the Passover meal, marks a shift in the Master's ministry. For more than three years He showed himself to the world, reaching out to unlovely men and women, performing miracles, revealing the Father in ways both large and small. Now the Cross was less than 24 hours away, and Jesus focused full attention on His disciples. They would carry His gospel throughout the world, therefore they must clearly grasp the basic truths about Him and His purpose for their lives.

How will Jesus teach these important themes? He could tell them—that would be "good" communication; or He might show them—that would be "better." But the lessons to be taught in the Upper Room required "best" communication, so the Lord appealed to both eyes and ears. He demonstrated truth in action, then He told them exactly what He wanted them to do.

Christ Was a Servant

The demonstration came first. While the meal was in progress, Jesus "rose from table, laid aside his garments, and taking a towel, tied it round him. Then he poured water into a basin, and began to wash his disciples' feet and to wipe them with the towel" (John 13:4-5).

After completing this lowly task, Jesus went back to the table and talked about the meaning of His action. He said, "'I have set you an example: you are to do as I have done for you. . . . a servant is not greater than his master, nor a messenger than the one who sent him. If you know this, happy are you if you act upon it'" (vv. 15-17). What message does this foot-washing Christ convey to the Twelve—and to us?

For one thing, Jesus was teaching a lesson about himself and His mission in the world. He employed a vivid object lesson to show the disciples that He had come from heaven to assume the role of servant in a needy world.

We have already seen that footwashing was a common courtesy, practiced by every good host in New Testament times. Paved streets were almost unknown in the ancient world, and footwear offered little protection against dust and mud. A person who walked any distance would need the services of a pitcher of water and a basin.

We also know that footwashing was considered a menial task, the work of a servant, rather than prominent men and women. Most people thought footwashing to be beneath their dignity, so they relegated the task to an underling.

Yet Jesus rose from the table, removed His seamless robe, poured water into a basin, and knelt to cleanse the dust-laden feet of His disciples. The scepter of universal sovereignty had been His to hold, yet He chose to lay aside His glory for a time. He who deserved the service of mankind stepped into a world of time and space to become a servant—that was the picture of himself that He wanted to stamp on the thinking of His men, just before He went to the Cross.

Apparently the followers of Jesus got the point, for the writings of the apostles emphasize the doctrine of the Incarnation—that God took the form of flesh and became a servant in the person of Christ. Paul puts it like this:

"For the divine nature was his from the first; yet he did not think to snatch at equality with God, but made himself nothing, assuming the nature of a slave. Bearing the human likeness, revealed in human shape, he humbled himself, and in obedience accepted even death—death on a cross" (Phil. 2:6-8).

Jesus came to earth to minister as a Servant, but He has now returned to heaven to enjoy His former glory. The Master showed this side of His character by once more dressing in His robe and taking His place at the table. In the hush of that Upper Room, the Twelve pondered the object lesson their Lord had just taught them about His person.

Most of us accept the doctrine of Christ's deity as fact. We recall phrases from the historic creeds of the church, and if pressed a bit, we can quote Bible verses about Jesus being the Son of God. But the footwashing Christ didn't rely on the "better" means of communication, He used the "best." He not only demonstrated His message but employed words to make His meaning clear. When the meaning gets through to us, we often feel it nipping our consciences.

"'If I, your Lord and Master, have washed your feet, you also ought to wash one another's feet,'" declared Jesus (John 13:14). His words stung the disciples, who had come to this final meeting with Jesus, arguing about who should occupy the most prominent places in His kingdom.

The men came into the Upper Room, glancing perhaps at the water in the pitcher and the towel, but not willing to make the first move. Nobody took up the pitcher and basin, and nobody reached for the towel. Since each of the men wanted to be first, none would consent to be last, to give in to the others and perform the lowly duty of washing another's feet. At last, Jesus made His move.

Are We Servants?

Are we, like the disciples, so preoccupied with our own goals that we fail to see the needs of people around us? Are we numbered among those whom William Barclay accuses of "standing on their dignity when they ought to be kneeling at the feet of their brethren"?[1]

Where are the men and women who take seriously the Master's call to be a servant of others? Some of them are found overseas, using their skills to fight poverty and human suffering, as well as preaching the gospel. Most of us know at least one dedicated professional who has exchanged the relative comfort of life in the Western world for multiple hardships in a developing country. Compared to the States, the hours may be long, the pay low, and working conditions primitive, yet this individual seldom engages in self-pity. The focus is always on ministry, the goal is to love Christ by serving others.

But modern "footwashing" isn't limited to overseas service. Visit any major city in North America and you will meet people who are volunteering their professional training on behalf of less fortunate men, women, and children. Perhaps you know a doctor, lawyer, or pastor who has chosen to live in a blighted neighborhood and touch people at their points of need. Maybe you are acquainted with a counselor or dentist who donates many hours a week to help physical or emotional hurts.

In Oklahoma City, a Christian center offers free medical and dental care to residents who come to the offices on Monday and Thursday nights. Physicians, lab technicians, registered nurses, and other helpers care for as many as 75 people each evening. Volunteer pharmacists fill up to 150 prescriptions during the three hours the clinic is open.

Ed Onley, who directs church community ministries for the Capital Baptist Association in Oklahoma City, demonstrates the mind-set of a Christian who has the servant attitude. "We find a need and then check to see if it is being met, even marginally, by our churches, another denomination, or even the government," he explains. "If it's not, we do everything we can to try and meet that need."[2]

Onley's rare gift for recognizing needs and then devising ways to meet those needs can be seen in numerous service projects. One day, while driving along an interstate highway, he saw a woman thumbing for a ride. A few minutes later he saw another woman with a child, standing beside the road. He had never before seen a woman hitchhiking, but an idea began to form in Onley's mind. Before long, Capital Baptist Association agreed to start a Women's Center, which specializes in ministry to transients.

In Douglasville, Ga., Buddy Bell spends many hours a week in the county jail, helping inmates with personal problems. Buddy preaches occasionally and holds Bible classes, but those aren't his primary duties. Most of the time he is carrying messages to relatives on the outside, giving haircuts, finding practical ways to befriend the lawbreakers. It isn't unusual for him to take prisoners to Sunday services and Sunday dinner at his home. He explains his concern in a few words:

"When I accepted the Lord, I agreed to tell people about the Savior. I've got an obligation from Him, and I'm telling people what He means to me." Buddy is crippled in both legs from polio, a condition that has confined him to a wheelchair. Nevertheless, he just keeps rolling along, "washing feet" in the tradition of his Master.

Or take the case of a 60-year-old Sunday School teacher who bought a pair of guinea pigs and began a systematic study of their feeding and care. A hobby? Not really. The teacher had tried again and again to win a certain boy in his class to Christ. He had failed, but love is ingenious and resourceful. When the man found that the boy kept guinea pigs, he took up the chore for the single purpose of reaching and winning the young fellow for the Lord. It was the teacher's way of "taking a towel."

To be a servant means that one takes a church office, not as a stepping-stone to a more prestigious post, but as a ministry to bless that part of the Body of Christ.

To be a servant may mean teaching a class of squirming boys and girls, taking care of a bedridden relative, or calling on someone in need.

To be a servant means to analyze a situation, ask "What would Jesus do?" then take practical steps in response to the answer.

"Footwashing" takes a thousand different forms in today's world, but each task carries a costly price tag. The kind of love Jesus demonstrated in the Upper Room is always sacrificial for the giver. Sometimes the action called for will cost us money, on other occasions the sacrifice may involve blocks of time or whittle away at our dignity.

Many lowly footwashing jobs are menial tasks from which we shrink, but we must keep our eyes on Christ when we are tempted to run away from duty. It wasn't beneath His dignity to put on the garments of a common slave and dirty His hands in the service of others. Is it beneath ours?

Members of a middle-class congregation never forgot the sermon their pastor preached from John 13. At one point, the minister described an imaginary visit to a museum in the New Jerusalem. He told about the objects on display: a widow's mite, the feather of a little bird, a handful of nails and thorns, and a common drinking cup that occupied an honored place.

Then he asked the attendant, "Don't you have a basin and towel in your collection?"

The attendant replied, "Not here. You see, they are in constant use."

There is a note of rebuke as well as splendor in the answer. Are the basin and towel in constant use—by us?

My Personal Encounter with Jesus

Am I conscious of the Lord calling me to some hidden, backroom job "serving tables," when I would rather occupy the limelight? Is He calling me to spend time and emotional energy on someone who is lonely? On someone who has a problem and needs my friendship?

If I am to take this encounter with Jesus seriously, what should be my next move?

My Prayer

Lord, it's so easy for me to seek ministry for myself when You want me to concentrate on offering ministry to others. I want to be a servant, but I have a feeling that it won't be comfortable; that I'll pull back at the last minute from those dirty, smelly "feet." Be patient with me, Lord, but don't let me duck responsibility. Keep pushing that basin and towel in front of me until I get on my knees and wash those feet. Amen.

Notes

CHAPTER 1

1. Graham Greene, *The Heart of the Matter* (New York: Viking Press, 1948), p. 235.

CHAPTER 2

1. Leon Morris, *The Gospel According to St. Luke* (Grand Rapids: Wm. B. Eerdmans Publishing Co., 1974), p. 147.

2. Article in "People" column, *Moody Monthly,* September 1979, p. 13.

CHAPTER 5

1. Halford E. Luccock, *365 Windows* (New York and Nashville: Abingdon Press, 1960), pp. 13-14.

CHAPTER 6

1. Elisabeth Elliot, "Key to Guidance," *Eternity,* June 1973, p. 27.

CHAPTER 7

1. From *Moody Monthly,* June 1979, pp. 17-18.

2. From "Master, the Tempest Is Raging," words by Mary A. Baker.

CHAPTER 8

1. James Kennedy, *The God of Great Surprises* (Wheaton, Ill.: Tyndale House Publishers, 1973), p. 15.

2. James C. Hefley, *Searchlight on Bible Words* (Grand Rapids: Zondervan Publishing House, 1972), pp. 79-82.

CHAPTER 11

1. Sidney M. Jourard, *The Transparent Self* (New York: Van Nostrand Reinhold, 1971), p. 6.

2. Francis Schaeffer in *Reaching All,* ed. Paul Little (Minneapolis: World-Wide Publications, 1974), p. 139.

3. F. F. Bruce, *The New Testament Documents: Are They Reliable?* (Chicago: InterVarsity Press, 1960), p. 15.

CHAPTER 12

1. William Barclay, *The Gospel of John,* vol. 2 (Philadelphia: Westminster Press, 1956), p. 162.

2. *World Mission Journal,* Southern Baptist Brotherhood Commission, February 1981, pp. 6-7.